Looking at Looking

About the Cover. Diego Velasquez's great painting *Las meninas* is a fascinating study of "people watching." The mysterious man in the background seems to be watching the others but also wondering if he is being watched himself. He *is,* of course—by *us.* Meanwhile, to the left, Velasquez watches King Philip of Spain and his queen as they, in turn, watch their children and maids. We know the artist is watching the royal couple because we can see their faces in the mirror on the opposite wall. *Or* is the artist watching *us* (watching him or them)? He at least seems to be watching us, for the simple reason that we can see that his pupils are centered within the circular whites of his eyes. But maybe it's not so "simple": Most of those whites are hidden by his eyelids, and so, it would seem, we can't *see* those "circles" at all!

At any rate, in everyday life, seeing "who is watching whom," including who is watching you, is socially important, *but,* as you will see in this book, there is much more than that to "looking at looking."

Looking at Looking

An Introduction to the Intelligence of Vision

Editor

Theodore E. Parks

With Contributions by:
Irvin Rock • John M. Kennedy
Richard L. Gregory • Ulric Neisser • Ross H. Day

Cover image is property of "El Museo Del Prado" owners of original painting,
jpg image provided by http://www.SpanishArts.com

Sage Publications, Inc.
International Educational and Professional Publisher
Thousand Oaks ■ London ■ New Delhi

For information:

Sage Publications, Inc.
2455 Teller Road
Thousand Oaks, California 91320
E-mail: order@sagepub.com

Sage Publications Ltd.
6 Bonhill Street
London EC2A 4PU
United Kingdom

Sage Publications India Pvt. Ltd.
M-32 Market
Greater Kailash I
New Delhi 110 048 India

Printed in the United States of America

Library of Congress Cataloging-in-Publication Data

Main entry under title:

Looking at looking: An introduction to the intelligence of vision /
edited by Theodore E. Parks.
  p. cm.
 ISBN 0-7619-2204-0 (pbk. alk. paper)
 1. Visual perception. 2. Visual communication. 3. Human information
processing. 4. Image processing. I. Parks, Theodore E. II. Title.
 BF241 .L64 2000
 152.14–dc21   00-009062

01 02 03 04 05 10 9 8 7 6 5 4 3 2 1

Acquiring Editor:	Jim Brace-Thompson
Editorial Assistant:	Anna Holland
Production Editor:	Diane S. Foster
Editorial Assistant:	Victoria Cheng
Typesetter/Designer:	Danielle Dillahunt
Cover Designer:	Michelle Lee

CONTENTS

To Samuel and Marian, Glenn, and,
in loving memory, Georgia

ACKNOWLEDGMENTS

I wish to thank the staffs of the Departments of Psychology at the University of California in Davis and at the University of Canterbury in Christchurch, New Zealand, for their many efforts—particularly those of Barbara Scoggins—in the production of the manuscript of this book. And, especially, I owe much thanks to Martha Todd Parks for her patient encouragement and invaluable assistance.

LIST OF REVIEWERS

Gregory Burton
Department of Psychology
Kozlowski Hall
Seton Hall University
South Orange, NJ 07079-2696

Stanley Coren
Department of Psychology
University of British Columbia
2136 West Mall
Vancouver, Canada V6T 1Z4

Lawrence K. Cormack
Department of Psychology
330 Mezes Hall
University of Texas
Austin, TX 78712

Gregory Lockhead
Department of Psychology
Duke University
227 Soc-Psych
Box 90086
Durham, NC 27708

Mark Tippens Reinitz
Psychology Department
Boston University
Boston, MA 02215

PREFACE

Despite war and political campaigns and the divorce rate, we all think of humans as intelligent. But is our *vision* intelligent? Is there anything "intelligent" about our ability to merely look at the world?

This question is important to many of us who study vision because intriguing suggestions that there may be an affirmative answer, of any sort, are an important part of what fascinates us about seeing. And there is also a curiosity here: This same possibility may be why it has proven to be so hard to provide that most intelligent of machines, a computer—much less a free-roaming robot—with "human" vision. Of course, any computer is really only as intelligent as its programmers know how to tell it to be. So what sort of a hint is that about us—about the cleverness of the human visual system or about our not-quite-clever-enough use of computers?

But why even bring up the notion of intelligence? After all, when we open our eyes, the world of objects and people before us simply "flows in"—or so it *seems*. That "seems" is important; the failure to produce "computers that see" is probably because of the fact that ordinary seeing is *not* at all simple. To our team of experts, the outstanding achievements (and *failures*) of vision reveal a highly complex, but fascinating, aspect of ourselves that most of us most of the time take for granted. *And* they make it fun.

Before turning to their ideas, however, those of you who are not yet involved in professional psychology may wonder about the form this book takes, so I should explain. It is inspired by two very different books. The first was the product of a typical psychological "convention," a meeting to which several psychologists brought and presented prewritten papers. These papers were then polished a bit and combined into a very satisfying book: Susan Petry and Glenn E. Meyer's *The Perception of Illusory Contours* (1987). It had, however, one flaw: Virtually all the comments we made, or could have made, about each other's ideas in the face-to-face situation were missing from the book.

The second book, Maurice Hershenson's *The Moon Illusion* (1989), has more of the flavor of a live interchange, even though, ironically, we various authors never actually met. Instead, several notable experts were asked to write a chapter on their findings and thoughts; these chapters were then distributed by mail to the rest of us so that we could write responses. The trouble with this approach, good as it was, was that it was difficult to keep track of so many main authors.

Benefiting from these experiences, I imagined the "staging" of the present book as a sort of miniature convention by mail. I asked three key theoreticians to each write an initial "core" chapter in isolation, much as people typically write papers beforehand to take along to read at a convention—hoping for the best and wondering what other speakers will say and how one's own efforts will be received. I must confess to editing these chapters in spots to abridge any point in a later chapter that had already been made in someone else's earlier chapter, much as a person at a convention would self-censor any point that turned out to be redundant.

Next, I asked a pair of experts to play the "audience" and to comment on the three "talks," trying especially to draw out areas of agreement and to weigh the importance of divergent points and the possibility of even further consensus. The latter, of course, is the road to progress that makes all of this worthwhile. Finally, I awarded myself the last word on all that had gone before.

In addition to their chapters in Part I, which form the central part of this book, each of the main authors provided some additional thoughts called "further looks," found in the back. The difference between the two is one of "level": The former are analogous to an address delivered to a general campuswide audience, whereas the latter are a bit more specialized and technical. As a result, a brief, but well worthwhile, reading assignment might omit those latter chapters. For instance, the first six chapters might be assigned alone as an opening assignment in an upper-division course in sensation and perception to gather the students' attention and motivate them to tackle later assignments in the larger, central textbook.

This plan satisfied me, but the real issue—its success—is left to the "gentle reader." Credit for the success of each chapter must go, of course, to its author.

INTRODUCTION

A Definition

A brief definition of *intelligence* might be useful. Since most or all *technical* definitions are not appropriate here (and "Intelligence is what intelligence tests measure" is worse), I turned instead to *Webster's New Collegiate Dictionary* (1956) and came up with this:

> 2. The power of meeting any situation, esp. a novel situation, successfully—also, the ability to apprehend the interrelationships of presented facts in such a way as to guide action.

Now *apprehend* is meant, I'm sure, in the mental sense of thoughtful understanding by the intellect, but it's fun to revert instead to an older meaning,

> 1. *Obs.* To seize

or to the near synonym, "to grasp." Alternatively, one might go to the modern meaning that has developed from "seize"— that is, "to arrest," or its near synonym, "to capture."

All in all, then, the emphasis is on *flexibility, activity,* and *purpose.* (Notice, also, that *learning* is not explicitly mentioned one way or the other. So, saying that vision is intelligent is not the same as saying that we quickly *learn how to see* or even that we learn to see *at all.* Maybe we do, maybe we don't. *Or* maybe, partly some of each.)

PART I

Our "Speakers"

The authors of the three "talks" that open this book were asked to ponder the possibility that at least some of the accomplishments of our visual systems might reasonably be called intelligent and to illustrate their arguments with vivid and fascinating examples of "vision in action."

IRV ROCK is famous for a long and distinguished career spent thinking about and investigating an amazing variety of questions about vision—in many cases, questions that the rest of us didn't realize were there! With a modesty that is so typical of him, he told me that he welcomed this chance (coming many years after the publication of his influential book *The Logic of Perception,* 1983) to review that career: What, after all those thoughts and experiments, could he hold to be reasonably certain?

I

STUPID PERCEPTIONS?

IRVIN ROCK

University of California at Berkeley

Right at the outset, I must admit that there are many difficult problems to be faced in taking the position that I will outline here: that perception is intelligent. For one, despite what most laypeople think, in many cases, perception is relatively immune from the effects of what we *know* about the scene in front of us. For example, illusions do not disappear when we find out they are illusions. In fact, some people may take this fact as a sign of the stupidity of perception because, here, perception seems to be rigid and inflexible, hardly a hallmark of intelligence. Many people see an absurdly long horse in Figure 1.1 even though we know that such an object is unlikely, and, indeed, the remainder of the pattern shows only normal horses. This does not seem very intelligent! Yet, even so, I will argue that the perception of the highly improbable long horse in Figure 1.1 *is* the result of intelligent processing.

AMODAL COMPLETION

But, first, there is another intriguing thing about this horse: It is an example of what is referred to as *amodal perception*. Amodal perception means that we perceive something in the *absence* of the relevant sensory stimulation—in this case, the absence of an image in our eyes of the central portion of the horse.

The brain supplies or "fills in" this missing stimulus. The very illuminating point of this is that our visual experience obviously includes *more* than just the patterns of light presented to our eyes. In a sense, we see more than "what's there," these amodal bits being added extras. You may very well think that our *eyes* are like cameras, but our *brains* certainly are not.[1] Moreover, examples of amodal additions abound.

The way that the incomplete circles in Figure 1.2 (p. 6) appear to be complete circles (partly covered by an illusory triangle) is also an example of amodal completion. Our perception is shot through with such amodal completion, as you can see by glancing at any room or outdoor scene. Because objects are almost always opaque, they will necessarily hide parts of other objects that are farther away. Yet these more distant, partially occluded objects are seen in their entirety rather than as only partial or truncated. The truth of this description is borne out by the difference in the appearances of the man in Figure 1.3a and 1.3b (p. 7). The man behind the desk in 1.3b appears to be complete in some sense even though in some other sense we do not "see" all of him. He certainly doesn't look like the truncated figure in 1.3a.

A brilliant demonstration by A. S. Bregman is shown in Figure 1.4a (Rock, 1995). It looks like a jumble of fragments. Now look at Figure 1.4b (p. 8). You will see several capital *B* letters in varying orientations covered by a rather strange blue ink-blot configuration with holes in it. However, the visible parts of the Bs are exactly the same as those in 1.4a, as you can see by examining

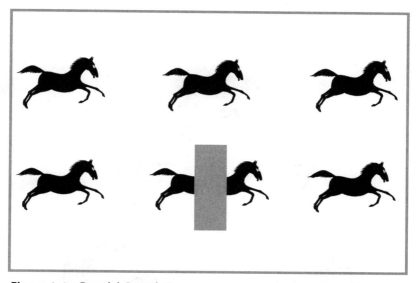

Figure 1.1. Amodal Completion

SOURCE: Adapted from *Perception,* I. Rock, Scientific American Library. Used with permission.

the two figures carefully. Why are the letters so easily perceivable in 1.4b when they are not in 1.4a?

There seem to be several factors at work here, but undoubtedly the major factor is that the blue "blobs" in 1.4b allow for completion and amodal perception of the letters. This blue covering allows for the completion of the fragments because they can be interpreted as being partially hidden. A more subtle point about this is that *all* the contours of the fragments in 1.4a "belong" to each fragment, whereas in 1.4b, the *end* contours of each fragment *do not* belong to the fragment. Rather, they are assigned to, or are seen as part of the edge of, the blue covering object. This is a matter of what is called "figure-ground organization."

The concept of figure-ground organization is so important for our understanding of perception that it warrants clarification.

Figure 1.2. An Illusory Triangle

Many psychologists who do not specialize in perception and most people who are not psychologists but have heard something about "figure and ground" believe that the distinction refers to an object (figure) that stands out from the background (ground). This description is correct, *but* it leaves out an essential further meaning of these terms. That is, any *border* between regions of different lightness or color can only belong to *one region or the other* at any given moment. As a result, the side to which it is "assigned" by

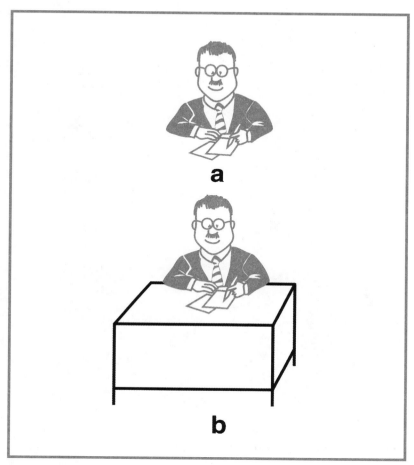

Figure 1.3. "Everyday" Completion

the brain (such that it perceptually belongs to that side) has a particular shape, whereas the other side is not shaped by that edge and appears to continue (amodally) behind the figure.

In the case of Figure 1.4b, the fragments are each clearly incomplete and are seen to go under the blue object, whereas the

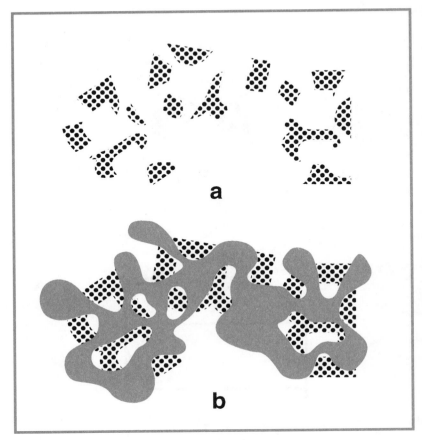

Figure 1.4. The Importance of the Occluder

fragments in 1.4a are all complete. Moreover, since complete-ness is not present, it is easier to relate the contours of the separate fragments to one another. One might say that the blue covering tells the observer to look for completions across them.

At any rate, this illustration is another striking demonstration of the reality of amodal perception since the same fragments look so different in 1.4a and 1.4b and yet are literally the same.

The blue covering object offers *stimulus support* for the amodal completion. Without it, even if we look back at 1.4a knowing what fragments go together, we *still* cannot see complete letters.

LOCAL DETERMINATION

To return now to the example of the improbable horse (Figure 1.1), we must deal with the question of why it is perceived since not only is it the kind of object never experienced, but it is embedded among a series of normal-length horses, which ought to add to the unlikelihood that the rectangle is occluding an abnormally long horse. Why, then, don't we see two amodal but normal parts of horses—the rear part of one and the front part of another—since this is presumably what is covered by the rectangle in the picture? There are several reasons why we do not and, instead, see a single elongated horse.

First, the expectation that we ought to perceive a *probable* object is based on the belief that perception is governed by what we know about the world. But the fact is that, by and large, this belief is false. Knowledge that we have acquired in the form of consciously held propositions and concepts, such as the size of horses, rarely affects how they appear. As I said at the outset, illusions of all kinds attest to this since, quite often, an illusion is a perception that we know not to represent the reality. So this is not what I mean by intelligence in perception; perception generally seems to be autonomous and insulated from knowledge.

Second, let us consider the expectation that we ought to perceive two horses of normal length in Figure 1.1 because of the context of the pattern as a whole, in which there are many horses of normal length. It is a truism about perception that context often *does* exert a strong influence on what we perceive. An interesting relevant example is shown in Figure 1.5.

In 1.5a, one perceives a rectangle occluding another (partly amodal) rectangle. But, in 1.5b, one may perceive the upper-right region as an *L* rather than as a partly hidden rectangle. Clearly, then, the context of the three other L regions affects the outcome, in part because of the symmetry of the whole configuration that is achieved if the upper-right region *is* seen as an L.

But against the effects of context is another powerful factor, what one might call "local determination." This refers to the fact that what is present in a given local region will exert a powerful effect on how that region and regions next to it are perceived. In fact, this sort of influence can be so strong that *some* of the time—or, for some observers, *all* of the time—the upper right L region in Figure 1.5b *will* be perceived as an occluded rectangle.

A good example of local determination is shown in Figure 1.6 and is referred to as an "impossible figure." In the figure, each of the cylinder-like regions on the bottom clearly represents a *solid object,* but, on the top, one of these looks like the *space between* two solid objects. By covering each region (top or bottom) alternately, two very different situations can be perceived. This is precisely because there is a conflict of local determination such that, overall, the drawing cannot represent any unified real object.

There are many other examples of local determination in perception. One is the basis for the impression of amodal completion behind an occluding object. In Figure 1.7a, one perceives a white stripe figure behind a blue rectangle. The local determination here concerns the junction of vertical and horizontal contours in the middle. One such junction is isolated in 1.7b. In this junction, segments ii and iii can appear to be one continuous line or edge, and segment i can appear to be a line or edge that goes under or behind the ii-iii edge. This impression is, of course, clearer in 1.7a, where the information from the other junctions and other contours provides further support for it. In particular, the sameness of direction of one of the line segments on the right side of the blue rectangle (ii) strongly supports the impression that both i and ii go behind the rectangle.

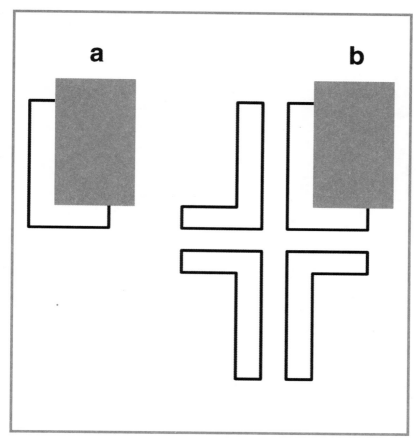

Figure 1.5. The Importance of Context

We have here a factor concerning "grouping" (or what goes with what), uncovered by the Gestalt psychologists, referred to as "good continuation." Not only is line ii grouped with line iii, and thus seen as one continuous longer line, but line i is grouped with line ii on the other side of the blue rectangle; both groupings happen on the basis of the principle of good continuation. In fact, Philip Kellman and Thomas Shipley (1991) have recently specifically suggested that the contours that are grouped behind

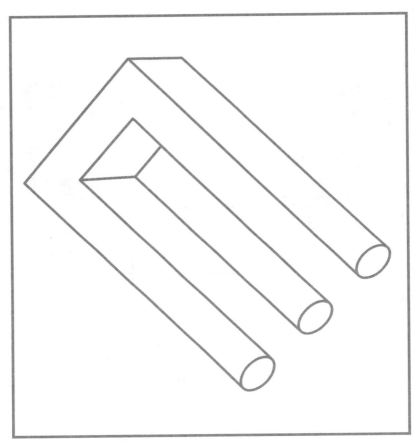

Figure 1.6. An Impossible-Object Figure

an occluding surface do so to the extent that they are relatable in good continuation.

Still another factor apparent in Figure 1.7 is figure-ground organization. Line ii-iii is perceived as the edge of the blue rectangle figure, and as such it belongs to and gives shape to the rectangle. It does not at all belong to the region to its left, and, for

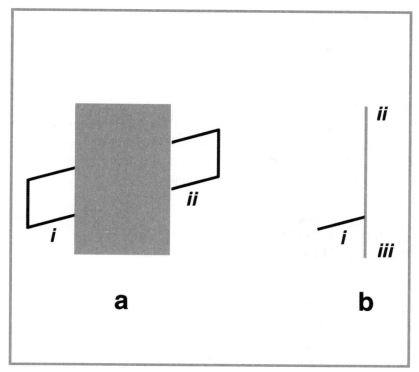

Figure 1.7. Local Determination of Occlusion

present purposes, this fact is particularly important in the region of the white stripe. Since the vertical contour in that region only belongs to the blue rectangle, the white region must be seen as going behind the blue rectangle. In other words, the white stripe has no terminating edge where it meets the side of the black rectangle.

So we see that a number of factors are responsible for the impression of the completion of an object that is perceived to be partially occluded by another object. These are all relevant to the example of the elongated horse in Figure 1.1. In that pattern, too, we have the same kind of local junctions as in Figure 1.7a. That means that, in Figure 1.1, the blue rectangle will be perceived *as such* because of the principle of good continuation in the region where it intersects with regions of the halves of the horse figure. This also means that the tops and bottoms of the two half-horse segments will be *connected* across by their relatability via good continuation. It also means that the rectangle preempts the contour in the vicinity of the horse fragments so that the left horse-half has no front contour *belonging to it,* and similarly for the rear contour of the right horse-half.

COGNITIVE INTELLIGENCE VS. PERCEPTUAL INTELLIGENCE

So, many factors provide powerful information for the perception of a partially amodal long horse behind a rectangle, improbable as this may be from the standpoint of our knowledge about horses. To repeat, perception follows its own laws, and, as a result, we may perceive improbable things. But that does not refute my claim that perception is intelligent. The intelligence of perception is different from that of conscious thinking based on knowledge of the world.

The Ames Room

I want to emphasize this last assertion with another example. Figure 1.8 represents how a very peculiarly built room appears to an observer who is standing in a particular place in the room. Of course, it looks like an ordinary room, but in fact it is not. That is, unbeknown to the observer, the height of the rear wall on the left is greater than that on the right. However, that left corner is *also* farther away from the observer, since the rear wall is slanted

Figure 1.8. A Sketch of an Ames Room

away in the third dimension. The two abnormalities of the rear wall—namely, the greater height of its left side and its greater distance from the observer—exactly *compensate* one another, with the result that, from one position of the viewer's eye, that rear wall projects a *rectangular* image to the retina. Two illusions result: The rear wall appears to be rectangular, and it appears to be at a right angle to you rather than slanting away. This is possible because we only let the observer use one eye, thus leaving him or her no depth cues to the built-in distortions. This effect was created by Adelbert Ames Jr. in 1951 and is known as the "Ames room." There is an Ames room in the Exploratorium in San Francisco.

Experiencing this illusion of a normal room, given its actual sever abnormality, is quite dramatic in itself, but there are other striking illusions that can be generated by this room. One is to place two people of roughly equal height against the rear wall, one to the left and one to the right. They will appear to be very different in size. An amusing supplementary effect can be achieved by requiring the individuals to exchange places by walking slowly in opposite directions along the rear wall until they each arrive at the opposite corners. As they walk along, one individual seems to shrink a great deal and the other seems to "grow before our eyes!"

At any rate, these illusions fly in the face of much that we know about the real world, such as the fact that people *do not* change size in a matter of seconds. The observer can even first view the room from the side, and thus see what its shape actually is, but this knowledge has essentially no effect on the illusions when the observer resumes viewing the room with one eye from the right spot.

Given cases like these, many investigators conclude that perception is hardly intelligent and is, in fact, inflexible and stupid. However, I want to emphasize that these "unlikely" perceptions do not violate a theory of perceptual intelligence. As I already noted above, perception is autonomous with respect to, and more or less insulated from, other modes of cognition such as thought. If, however, the nature of the process underlying the achievement of a given percept is based on inference and rule, then it is appropriate to consider such a process as intelligent. Now the Ames room illusion can indeed be accounted for in such a way. First, given no useful depth cues to the contrary, it is a "plausible" assumption on the part of the brain that the rear wall is in a place perpendicular to the line of sight. The rectangular image it produces supports that assumption. And given that perception, all the other illusions that occur in the room make sense.

For example, a person standing in the left rear corner is, in fact, farther away than a person in the right rear corner, so in Figure 1.8 she yields an image to the eye that is much smaller than that of the other person. However, she is not *seen* as being farther away, so the correct distance to her cannot be taken into account, and, therefore, that person will incorrectly be perceived to be abnormally small, much smaller than a person in the other corner. In this way, illusory shrinkage and growth also make sense. (The Ames phenomena are definitely something you ought to see for yourself. If you can't get to the Exploratorium or some other place that has an Ames room, it is well worth your taking a few minutes to follow a suggestion made to me by Ted Parks and make a much simplified, but still impressive, version for yourself, as described in Figure 1.9.)

Therefore, even though the dramatic change in the apparent size of the two people as they change places seems to have little to do with intelligence (and, in fact, seems to be very unintelligent if one views the outcome from the standpoint of conscious thinking based on acquired knowledge about the world), from the standpoint of intelligent processing—including the very important idea of *taking account* of distance in trying to see the size of something—one can regard the dramatic illusion of size change as a result of an intelligent process.

Rejection of Coincidence

However, in the case of the elongated horse, one may ask, Why is following principles such as good continuation intelligent? The answer requires somewhat of a digression from the ex-

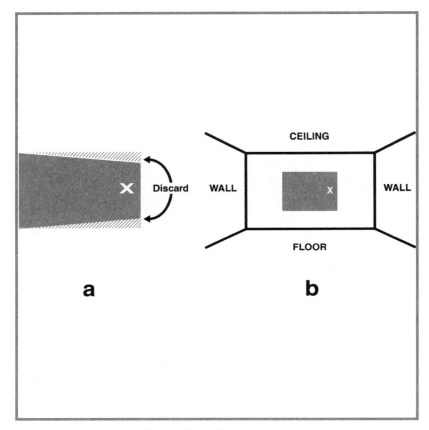

Figure 1.9. Your Own "Ames Room"

A rough Ames room can be made very simply and quickly by cutting away parts of an ordinary sheet of blank unlined paper (or, better, of poster stock) approximately as shown in 1.9a. Hold this with both hands several inches from your eyes while facing a wall several feet away. Now slowly angle the wide end *away* from yourself until the top and bottom edges are *parallel* to the floor and ceiling as pictured in 1.9b (about 45° should do). Now *close* one eye and compare the size of your hand that holds one end to the size of your other, but first try to "see" the paper as a rectangle. (If the paper is stiff enough, try releasing one end and moving that hand slowly toward the other.) The apparent effects on your anatomy should repay your trouble!

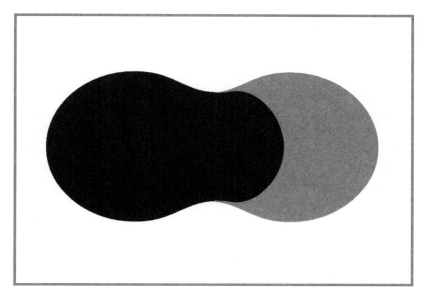

Figure 1.10. Rejecting Coincidences

amples we have been considering. The retinal image only very rarely will contain certain regularities of arrangement that are, for lack of better terms, coincidental or accidental—that is, regularities that *do not* derive from actual regularities in the objects or events in the scene itself. That fact has a good deal to do with how regularities will be seen. For example, suppose that, from a certain angle, the image of the borders of one object *just happens* to be perfectly aligned with the image of another object, as illustrated in Figure 1.10. Thus, although there are *two* entirely different objects (they are at different distances), from one particular viewing point, their borders yield retinal images that coincide as good continuations of one another. Now, if this were to occur, we might reasonably enough perceive them to belong to *one* object, or, rather, we might simply perceive one object instead of two. In doing so, the brain is rejecting pure coincidence and concluding that the good continuation of the contours in the retinal image implies one object in the world. Another way of stating this is that the perceptual system, like a good detective, rejects the conclusion that a coincidence has occurred in the eyes.

A further example would be the coincidence of two adjacent objects yielding images of exactly the same lightness, texture, and color. We would reject that regularity as being accidental uniformity and perceive one object rather than two. Camouflage makes use of this rule by rendering adjacent objects with very similar stimulus properties as one. That is, such contiguity implies unity and is experienced as such whether the connection is "real" or not. To do otherwise is to accept the contiguity as a coincidence. So when a light comes on or goes off just as a door is slammed, there is a tendency to experience one as the cause of the other. When one object moves and encounters another and that second object then moves away, we experience the former as causing the latter.

What all these examples serve to suggest is that various principles that the brain follows in arriving at a perception (or a "perceptual solution") are based on rejecting interpretations that would be based on a coincidental or accidental regularity within the retinal image. In following the principle of good continuation, for example, it is as if the perceiver is (unconsciously) thinking that the contours in the retinal image (from different objects) that are smooth continuations of one another are most likely to be delineating a single "thing" in the world. Otherwise, like a bad detective, one would be accepting an interpretation based on a most unlikely coincidence or accident of stimulation. As to the *origin* of such a principle or rule, it is most likely innate. It is a highly *adaptive* rule that surely would have had survival value by virtue of the rules of the physical world in which we have evolved. From this perspective, it is an intelligent, adaptive mode of perceptual processing.

INTELLIGENCE IN MOTION PERCEPTION

What about a type of perception I have not yet considered here although it occurs constantly in daily life: namely, the perception of movement? It is fashionable nowadays among investigators of perception to explain the perception of the motion of objects by the "firing" or discharging of neurons in the brain that respond to the movement of an image over the retina in the eye in a particular location. These cortical neurons are called motion detectors. It is indeed a fact, discovered by physiologists (D. H. Hubel and T. N. Weisel and others) by electrical recording from a single cell in the cortex of the brain, that such a cell will fire vigorously when the image of an edge of an object is moved back and forth over a certain location in the retina. Since that neuron will not respond to other kinds of stimulation of the retina in that location, it is appropriate to call that neuron a "detector" of motion.

Does this important, admittedly exciting, discovery explain the perception of motion? Hardly. Consider these facts: Whenever we move, or turn our head or just move our eyes, the images of all the stationary objects in the scene sweep over the retina. Thousands of motion detectors must be excited. But we don't see these stationary objects moving. So the mere excitation of a motion detector cell can hardly be a *sufficient* explanation of the perception of motion. It is perhaps a *necessary* condition. That is not correct either. Take the case of tracking a moving object with your eyes. If you succeed in tracking it, the object's image remains in *one place* on your retina: in the center of your vision, the fovea. Even in an otherwise totally dark room, you see the object move just as well even though no motion detectors are discharging. Obviously, then, such discharge is not a *necessary* condition for the perception of motion, either. In both cases—not perceiving motion of stationary objects when we move our eyes and perceiving motion when we track a moving object with our eyes—

the outcome is based on *taking account* of what the eyes are doing in *interpreting* the meaning of the behavior of the retinal image, whether that be motion or nonmotion.

Apparent Motion

We now come to another phenomenon of motion perception that I would like to discuss at greater length because I believe it to be an interesting example in which one can make out a good case for a "problem-solving" theory of vision. I am referring to the phenomenon known by various names in the field as apparent motion or stroboscopic motion or as the phi phenomenon. It is the phenomenon that gives us our perception of motion in moving pictures or television. As most people know, moving pictures result from a succession of still photographic frames. These frames move in front of the projector bulb one at a time and remain stationary for a brief period. Thus, if an actor's arm is in one position in Frame 1 and in a slightly different position in Frame 2, then one sees the arm moving when viewing the film.[2]

You may be interested to learn that this phenomenon of apparent motion was studied in a famous experiment by Max Wertheimer that launched the school of thought known as Gestalt psychology in 1912. Wertheimer created an apparent motion display in the laboratory by first presenting a stimulus such as a bright line in one place and then causing it to disappear and be replaced by a line in a different place and so on, back and forth. He found that the spacing and timing had to be just right to create the impression of motion; not just any timing would do. For example, if the time between lines is too great, say one half-second, one sees just a line here and then a line there but no motion. If the time is too short, then one sees both lines lit simultaneously (neural persistence) but no motion. Incidentally, what Wertheimer believed was important about this phenomenon of apparent motion was that there was no moving image in the stimulus. Therefore, there could be no sensation of motion caused by the stimulus. But the then-prevailing psychology believed that all perception reduced to sensations created by specific stimuli. Instead, to Wertheimer, it seemed that the explanation for the perceived motion must be an event in the brain. The motion was an example of the whole being different from the sum of its parts, a dictum that has long since been associated with Gestalt psychology.

Temporal Parameters of Apparent Motion

What, if anything, more can be said about the "why" of the specific timing required for apparent motion? As far as I can tell, most investigators have simply accepted this as a fact about the brain without offering any rationale. I would suggest that there is a rationale. First, consider the condition in which the rate of alternation is too rapid. Why does one see both objects as simultaneously "on" rather than as motion? We have already noted that neural persistence is relevant. Stimulus 1 is still visible when Stimulus 2 comes on. The reason why that state of affairs is anathema for apparent motion is really rather obvious. How, logically speaking, can Stimulus 1 have moved to the location of Stimulus 2 if it is still seen where it is? The condition simply doesn't fit the solution that Object 1 has moved to the position of Object 2.

The conditions of stimulation that *do* lead to the perception of motion are essentially these: At Time 1, an object appears in a certain location and then inexplicably disappears. I say "inexplicably" because, ordinarily in daily life, things disappear from view when other objects occlude them, such as when the other object moves in front or we move to the side. Things don't disappear otherwise except in rare instances such as a quickly dissipating puff of smoke or in a magic show. The next thing to happen in an apparent motion display is that the same shaped, sized, and colored object appears inexplicably in another nearby location. Again, "inexplicably" because in daily life things just don't appear suddenly with no explanation of where they came from. Usually, things appear that were not visible a moment before only when an object in front no longer covers it, as when it or we move. The brain is faced with an unusual problem: namely, how to explain the inexplicable appearance of an object in one place, its inexplicable disappearance, its inexplicable reappearance in another place, and so forth. Perceiving a single object *moving* is a good solution.

Given this background, we can now ask why apparent motion breaks down if the time interval between presentations is too great. Such a long time interval would have the effect of slowing down the motion. Why should that destroy the illusion of motion (and, after all, it is an illusion!)? I would suggest the following reason. If the movement is very slow, one would expect to see the object moving across *between* Place 1 and Place 2. But since it doesn't move across, the failure to see it doing so is strong evidence against the hypothesis that it is moving. By contrast, at a faster rate—one at which apparent motion does appear—we do not expect to see the object moving across. Why is that? Because with fast movement of objects that actually do move, all we see at best is a *blur* between the end positions.

The Lessons of Apparent Motwion

First of all, apparent motion may be related to a very fundamental feature of perception: the tendency on the part of the perceptual system to make assumptions, in this case to assume the continued existence of objects in the world. After all, we often look away from objects, and, when we look back, we certainly expect them to be there. We would be surprised indeed if they were not. Experiments have been performed attesting to this fact (although it is claimed that, in children below 6 months of age, this "object permanence" feature of adult perception is not yet present). So one might interpret our experiments on apparent motion to mean that the object-permanence solution (that the one object is present, but moving, all the time) wins out. The power of the perceptual assumption of permanence is impressive: Apparent motion is all but irresistible. Try *not* seeing motion in a movie, even in a silent-era "flicker"!

Second, given all the reasons I have advanced for the inadequacy of a physiological motion-detector explanation of apparent motion, one might well ask what the purpose is of such "detectors." Why did a brain evolve to include these specialized cells? A reasonable answer might be that the activity of these cortical cells informs us that a contour is moving over the retina in a particular location. In some cases, such neural activity would correctly signal that an object in a particular place in the scene was moving, but in other cases it would not. In other words, these detectors would serve at a low-level stage of processing to inform about what was happening *in the retina.* From this perspective, the discharging of such cells is not directly an *object*-moving detector but, rather, a *retinal*-image motion detector. However, I hasten to remind you that even the low-level detection is not necessary for the perception of motion, given all the examples above in which movement is perceived when nothing is moving across the retina.

This is perhaps an appropriate moment to make a general point about how many contemporary investigators theorize about perception. They start with a physiological discovery—such as that of single-cell motion detection—and then try to apply it as an explanation to what we know about the corresponding phenomena or try to accommodate the facts to fit the discovered mechanism. Although this might be a reasonable way to proceed in some cases, it often is a bad way to proceed. Instead, one should look at the range of facts one wishes to explain (e.g., facts bearing on the perception of movement) and *then* try to come up with an explanation of the *kind of mechanism* that would explain them, setting aside what we might already know about how the brain works. This allows more freedom in theorizing. Following that, one might infer what kind of brain event must occur to deal with the hypothesized mechanism and then proceed to look for it (or tell the neurophysiologists what they should be looking for). However, I want to correct any possible misinterpretation concerning my view about the brain as an explanation of perception (or of any other mental events for that matter). I believe, as do virtually all investigators in psychology, that brain events cause all mental events. Some brain events have as a concomitant conscious mental events such as perceptions. The mental aspect is an emergent property of the neurophysiological process. So when I contrast an account of visual experience with a physiological theory, I do not mean to imply that my account is not based on brain events, only that a particular brain theory is premature and as such does not account for the facts.

PERCEPTUAL RATIONALIZATION

To return to our discussion of perceptual phenomena *per se,* illusory contour perception (see Figure 1.2) also illustrates a rejection of excessive coincidence. To begin with, there are dark fragments such as incomplete circles. Being surrounded objects, they are seen as figures in figure-ground organization. The central white region is perceived as ground. But the coincidental alignment of the borders of the wedgelike openings in the circles calls for an explanation. The perceptual system seeks good explanations for the *entire* stimulus array in addition to seeking to avoid acceptance of coincidental input to the eyes. So the brain "wants" to see these alignments (as well as, perhaps, the incompletenesses of the circles) explained. It can do so by reversing figure-ground in the central region. That region of what was the *ground* now becomes the *figure* (in the example, in the shape of a triangle), and the figure as a "thing" is opaque and can fully explain the alignments and incompletenesses. Therefore, I consider this outcome—that is, creating a figure of the central white region—as an example of "perceptual *rationalization*."

There is one other feature of the resulting perception that can also be thought of as an example of rationalization. Once the brain has constructed the covering central triangle by figure-ground reversal, it ought to have visible edges. But since the regions inside and outside of that triangle are equal in whiteness, there is no stimulus support for such phenomenal edges. Therefore, the brain *creates* the illusion that the inner triangle is whiter than the surrounding white. Now the edges are visible. From this perspective, the "lightness effect" that usually occurs along with the illusory contour phenomenon is an example of perceptual rationalization *par excellence* (Parks, 1989).

It is interesting that a phenomenon such as rationalization should occur in perception, since it occurs in so many other kinds of mental activity. Rationalization is best known in cases in which one tries to supply a more favorable explanation for one's actions when such actions are not deemed to be particularly creditable by oneself and others. But this popular meaning is somewhat different from the dictionary meaning of the term, which is to provide a rational basis for one's actions rather than simply a favorable one when the actions might otherwise appear to be irrational or without any explanation. A very good example of this is the case of a person enacting a posthypnotic suggestion. The suggestion might be, let us say, to sit down on the floor when the hypnotist gives a certain signal. When asking the subject why he or she did this, the subject will inevitably come up with a reason, such as "I thought I was about to faint" or "My leg began to hurt." We, the observers of the sequence of events, know that these explanations are not the true basis of the action. Apparently, the need to provide an explanation for what one does is very strong.

A different kind of rationalization occasionally occurs during dreaming when some external stimulus, such as a repetitive loud sound, "gets through" to the dreamer's consciousness. The dreamer then integrates this perception into the dream in some sensible way. Otherwise, it would remain unexplained.

The rationalizations that I am suggesting are ones that try to make sense of a stimulus structure or event that contains strong coincidences or that simply does not fit (or seemingly contradicts) the ongoing perception. As I mentioned, the lightness illusion we see in illusory figures is an excellent example of exactly such a case, and that fact—along with the fact that illusory figures are also very good examples of "stages" in perception (see my "Further Look" in Chapter 7)—goes far toward explaining their fascination for workers in vision. Along with many other phenomena, they point insistently to the problem-solving, and therefore *intelligent,* nature of our visual system.

NOTES

1. My use of the word *brain* requires explanation. In discussing psychological phenomena, investigators need to refer to some entity that is achieving the effect under consideration. Investigators of perception sometimes use the phrase "the perceptual system," and investigators of memory sometimes use the phrase "the memory system." It is presumably the processing that occurs in that "system" that explains the phenomenon. Alternatively, one might simply refer to the brain as the entity in which the processing occurs. And now that mental events have become more respectable with the demise of behaviorism, investigators will sometimes dare to refer to the "mind" as the entity in which the processing occurs. However, since all mental events are based on brain events, the formulation "mind/brain" or simply "brain" seems better to me. However, because of our very limited understanding of how brain

mechanisms can account for mental events, we often formulate our hypotheses and theories in language that is psychological rather than physiological.

2. Many people who are aware of this fact mistakenly believe that the complete explanation of movies has to do with what we might call neural persistence; that is, that we still see Frame 1 even after it has moved away from the projector's lens. That is true, or at least it is now true with the perfection of the timing of the projector (in the early years of motion pictures, one often perceived a flickering effect). But the reader, who may be one of those who thought that persistence explained the total phenomenon, should ask where does the *motion* come from? The persistence only explains why we do not perceive a blank gap between frames (and why early movies were called "flickers"). It does not explain the motion.

JOHN M. KENNEDY has always admired one of history's most original thinkers about vision, J. J. Gibson. However, as strongly as he has advocated the value of Gibson's ideas, his *own* very original book, *A Psychology of Picture Perception* (1974), not only went well beyond the scope of Gibson's interests but thoughtfully (and convincingly) questioned many of the things "we all know" about the psychological foundations of visual art. But more pertinent to our question: Is—and *how* is and to *what extent* is—vision intelligent to him?

2

SMART GEOMETRY!

JOHN M. KENNEDY

University of Toronto, Canada

How vision gives us awareness of the properties of distant objects, while usually avoiding important errors in our detecting machinery, is the central question of visual science. Interestingly, Denis Diderot, of France, in the late eighteenth century offered a faulty answer to the basic question. The flaws in his answer reveal just what kind of an answer the science of vision is in fact seeking.

DIDEROT AND GIBSON

Diderot proposed that the senses can give us only a few rather primitive, sketchy sensations (Morgan, 1977). He then was forced to ask himself how vision could turn these limited sensations into many varied impressions of objects and landscapes. His answer was a very curious one. He concluded that we probably compare the sensations with their causes—that is, with the objects and landscapes. This is quite an illogical theory, alas. In effect, Diderot is saying that we only have sensations to go on, but sensations can be converted to impressions of objects because, independently of the sensations, we also have awareness of the causes of the sensations. Diderot's account is *contradictory.* If we are indeed aware of the objects, then the objects must be causing that awareness and are not just causing a few primitive sensations. But what *does* allow the objects to cause that awareness? Diderot does not give the answer.

The American J. J. Gibson's response was astute. Gibson argued that vision allows much more than primitive sensations and that, to do so, perception uses *complex patterns.* That is, Gibson's genius lay in (a) his realization that there are complex patterns in the input to the senses and that these patterns are accurate indicators of the surroundings of the observer and (b) his suggestion that the visual system responds to these complex, accurate indicators with a percept. Diderot's error was to assume that we have only a few primitive sensations to go on; he then had to struggle to find an extra mechanism producing complex, varied percepts from those few sensations.

How Do We Do It?

To understand Gibson's claim, we have to understand what makes an indicator accurate. Gibson's solution was to point out that patterns are "distinctive." That is, the kind of pattern that comes from a tree does not come from a cloud, a mountain, a rock, an insect, a mammal, or any other kind of object in the natural environment. Indeed, there are no natural objects that are halfway between trees and mammals or trees and clouds. Light can be quite detailed—almost infinitely detailed, in fact—and the patterns from one kind of object contain distinctive features that do not arise from any other natural object.

How detailed can light be? How precisely are optic patterns related to the objects that are the sources of the light patterns? Consider a photograph taken in a Toronto classroom of 30 or so students, each with somewhat different clothes, hairstyles, coloring, faces, sizes, and so on. That photograph is unique to its time and place. Its exact copy could not be taken anywhere else in Toronto or Ontario or Canada or North America or the world or the solar system. It also could not have been taken, probably, at any other historical time in Toronto or Canada or the world—or probably the galaxy since the Big Bang.

Detail and distinctiveness are important characteristics of light and all the sensory patterns. They are the basis of information, as follows: A pattern can indicate its source if that pattern can come only from that source. In nature, a certain pattern indicates a tree (or a wolf or a river) if it is only present when there is indeed a tree (or a wolf or a river) in our surroundings. A pattern "specifies" a tree (and another pattern specifies a wolf, and a third specifies a river), we could say. Light is informative if it has this kind of "specificity." Sensory patterns are distinctive, and they specify particular sources in the environment of the observers.

Perception could indeed use a distinctive pattern of light, precisely because it comes from only one source. But how could a perceiver possibly know that a pattern is distinctive? First of all, it is amusing to realize that there is no opportunity for an observer to compare a pattern *even* with all the other patterns, present or past, to which the observer has been exposed. That would be an endless task (besides being utterly thankless).

More important, much the same point about the observer's limitations can be made in connection with the fact that a pattern indicates *some sort of thing* in the environment. The observer might try to spend some time checking on the implications of particular patterns—by exploring them in more detail, for example—but, by and large, we often have to act on the evidence of our senses without double-checking the evidence. For instance, we often drive down the road, since it looks safe, without double-checking in some indirect, extra fashion that the indications of safety are reliable. Indeed, any attempt by the observer to find a perceptual basis for checking the meaning of a perceptual pattern merely turns perception once again into a check on perception—the inescapable loop Diderot fought in vain to escape.

So while Gibson correctly indicates that perception can rely on enormously informative patterns, we must look further to find out how human observers can fathom the meaning of those patterns. It cannot be that particular patterns are found to be distinctive, after a lot of investigation, by the observer. And it cannot be that the observer generally discovers the meaning of patterns by checking them against something else. Rather, there must be something about many perceptual patterns that make it possible to apply some *general interpretative procedures* to them. In turn, those analytic methods must be based on general laws and common *geometries* in the world around us.

In effect, the fact that there is information in light in nature is the condition that has made it possible for vision to evolve to use general principles in reacting to light. The information is present in nature because of distinctiveness and specificity, but vision and the other perceptual systems have analytic principles built in and do not bother to check for distinctiveness or ascertain specificity. They merely determine what kinds of shapes are present in the input and produce a percept of the source.

The $64,000 question at this point, then, is what are those general principles? If vision does not operate with strategies for verifying that a pattern has specificity and distinctiveness—for proving that a pattern is informative—what principles are actually reflected in vision's operations?

TEXTURES AND GRADIENTS
SHOW SURFACES

An elegant example of Gibson's answer concerns the manner in which changes in texture can enable us to see a floor (carpet texture) meeting walls (wallpaper texture) and walls meeting a ceiling (stippled texture). A few scattered trees on a ski slope can give us an amodal impression of a continuous surface on which trees stand even if the snow itself is perfectly uniform. In Gibson's terms, vision responds to the "optic gradients" given by texture elements. Nearby elements project large, widely separated optic texture units. As the distance to the textured region increases, the elements project smaller and more densely packed optic texture elements. As shown in Figure 2.1, the result is a gradient from sparse to dense optic texture, which shows that the surface with the texture is continuous and recedes into the distance.

Technically speaking, the "optic gradient" is the rate of change of the density of optic texture. A flat receding surface has a constant rate of change of optic texture density. Where two surfaces meet, the gradient changes abruptly. A corner is an abrupt change (a discontinuity) in the rate of change of optic texture density. If we are close to a cliff edge, we see flat ground receding from us and then the cliff's edge and then, beyond the edge, the distant floor of a valley below. The optic texture at our eye would show a constant texture gradient corresponding to the flat ground on which we are standing and a second constant texture gradient corresponding to a flat valley floor. The cliff edge would be indicated by an abrupt change in the texture density. The wide elements of the nearby ground provide large texture units optically, and the valley floor provides small texture units, so the cliff edge corresponds to a discontinuity in the texture gradient.

A curved surface corresponds to a gradual change in the rate of change of texture. The optic texture gradient at the eye

Figure 2.1. The greater density of cacti as you move up the page indicates that they are on a flat plane at greater and greater distance (unless, of course, you're in a *very* strange "forest").

provided by the texture elements on a cylinder can gradually transform from very little gradient on the nearest part of the cylinder, to a more rapid gradient of change as the cylinder's surface begins to recede from the observer, and then to a maximum gradient when the surface's slope has a tangent through the observer's vantage point.

The scale on which vision is able to use texture units and their gradients successfully is limited. The result is, at times, quite surprising. For example, if we are looking at a ski hill in the distance, we may see it as very steep, almost a vertical wall. When we come close, we see it as having quite a gentle slope. The reason it looks very steep from a distance is that we use units of texture such as trees at the top and bottom of the hill to gauge the slope.

From a distance, the spaces between the trees at the top of the hill and those at the bottom may appear nearly the same to the eye. But if we are close to the bottom of the hill, the nearby spaces at the bottom of the slope may appear much larger than before. Those at the top will now *also* be closer than before, but still not very large. Thus, the *ratio* of the two sets will suggest a stronger slope.

Consider an observer looking into a 90° concave corner formed by a step. Imagine that the observer's eye is on the line bisecting the 90° corner (i.e., at 45° to the horizontal). The abrupt change in the texture gradient will be evident if the observer is reasonably close to the corner and the texture elements provide distinctly different angles. But, from afar, all the texture elements would be virtually uniform to the eye, and no corner would be evident. Instead, the corner would begin to resemble a flat surface to the observer (although possibly darker to one side than the other). Similarly, when viewing a cliff from an airplane, the cliff top's texture and the valley floor's texture will project nearly equal-sized optic texture units, and the cliff will often be very difficult to discern. Evidently, the scale of the scene matters a great deal when we are detecting slopes and steps.

It is important to understand that a white ski slope stretching between a few isolated trees may be providing virtually no useful texture details to the eye. Nevertheless, it can give us an amodal impression of a continuous slope joining the contour at the base of the trees. It is this continuous slope that changes from steep to gentle as we approach from afar. The trees appear to stand on the amodal slope. If there are flat patches on the slope, in addition to changing from large to small angular size, they will change their projected shape. For example, flat circular patches will project as circles when they are underfoot and as more and more extreme ellipses as they recede. If the patches always project as circles, they will appear to stand on the slope, like spherical boulders. In these cases, perception responds well to the *relationship* between the increasing distance and the changes that should be present in the projected shapes of objects on the receding surface.

THE FLOW AS THE OBSERVER MOVES

When the observer changes location in a textured environment, the direction of the texture elements changes. What was directly underfoot falls behind the moving observer. What was initially to the left or right and ahead of the observer moves farther to the side. Only an element that was exactly at the observer's heading keeps its direction unchanged. It is *invariant* in direction.

In Gibson's terms, the set of changes in direction as the observer moves gives rise to an "optic flow" (see Figure 2.2) as all the elements "stream by" the moving vantage point. The flow can give the observer a vivid impression of speed when he or she moves fast. The driver and passengers of a speeding car get a flowing, blurred impression from the texture elements on the road whizzing toward them. A similar impression can be obtained by viewing from an airplane window during take off, seeing the landing strip whooshing past.

It is interesting to note that, as an airplane takes off, it *increases* its speed as it climbs, yet many people get the impression that the airplane seems to be moving more *slowly*. Why is this? The answer is that vision often responds to change in angle per-unit-time when assessing apparent speed. If something changes its direction from us by 45° per second, and something else changes by 1° per second, vision assesses one as crawling by and one as shooting by. When taking off, the amount of angular change for each point on the level, solid ground varies according to its distance. The farther away the elements are, the less they change direction. Nearby elements move so rapidly that they may blur,

Figure 2.2. The arrows represent the "optical flow" you would see as you moved forward. *However,* this flow is so much a part of everyday experience that, for most of us, it is difficult to deliberately notice. A better idea is to try to notice the *reverse* flow that occurs when, for example, you look out of the *back window* of a rapidly moving car on a long straight stretch of road. Try it next time you can. (You can also experience this when you're driving by staring at the rearview mirror, but that is definitely *not* a "better idea.") When you are moving forward, the flow reflects *where you are going* (in this case, toward the "bull's eye").

while, later, others hardly change direction at all and give a very different impression of our speed. (By the same token, driving across a broad valley takes great patience if you persistently watch the horizon!) So, our accurate use of flow to experience speed depends on the presence of nearby objects and also on our attention to them. Nevertheless, that "invariant" flow—that flow that is the same for *all* objects on the ground at a particular speed and distance *no matter* what their texture—is important information.

Figure 2.2 also shows the set of changes of *direction* of flow. A point just above the horizon (the "invariant" point) is not moving

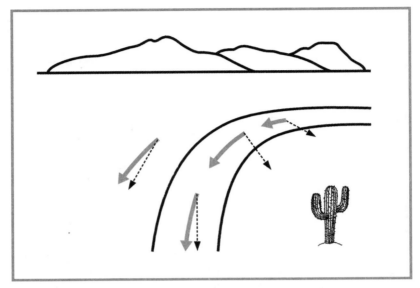

Figure 2.3. If you are driving *correctly* around a curve, the flow of the surface of the road will be centered on the edges of the road (solid arrows). If not, the flow will be different (e.g., the dashed arrows), indicating that you are about to go *off the edge!*

at all, which means that there is where we are headed. So this figure illustrates a second very useful property of optic flow: It tells us *where we are going* just as much as it gives us an impression of our speed.

If we wish to follow the curve of a road as we drive a car, we should turn the steering wheel until the flow takes on a curve that matches the curve of the road (see Figure 2.3). If we oversteer, the optic flow field will have a tighter curve than the road, and we will be in danger of running onto the inside shoulder of the road. If we understeer, the flow field will have a shallower curve than the road, and we will run onto the shoulder on the outside. The job of the driver is to match the flow field's curvature to that of the road (Warren, Mester, Blackwell, & Morris, 1991).

One fascinating aspect is that many drivers can accurately tell if they are understeering or oversteering but don't know what optic properties tell them where they are going. Also, we can see where we are going, but we are often at a loss about what to tell others (e.g., novice drivers) to look out for so that they can quickly learn to do the same.

Of course, this difficulty may be partly because we are responding to a very complex "invariance": the unvarying *relationship* between the *shape* of the optical flow and the *shape* of the road, regardless of the surface texture of the road and regardless of the specific curvature of this particular bend in it.

OPTIC FLOW AND RETINAL FLOW

Visual motion is not just a matter of direction from the observer. We gaze in particular directions, or our eyeballs may rotate to follow a moving element. As a result, two kinds of impressions can arise.

Consider a person riding as a passenger in a car moving along a straight, highly textured road surface. The ground texture is flowing toward him or her, radiating outward from the heading point, with the rate of change of the direction of each element depending on its distance from the observer. What is happening *visually*, however, depends on where that person's eyes are aimed. If he or she visually follows some element of the flowing texture, then visually that texture element remains *fixed* in the center of gaze. The passenger may be trying to determine if a mark on the road is a bump or a pothole. The mark is stuck in the same place on the person's retinas as long as his or her eyes follow that element. Evidently, there is a difference between the set of changes of direction from an observer's moving vantage point and the set of changes on the retinas that result when flowing texture is followed by the observer's eyes. (This is perfectly clear when you imagine for a moment that you are not moving but something else is—say a fly buzzing in front of you. The fly might go up, down, and around, changing its direction from your vantage point. But if you follow the fly, keeping it in the center of gaze—on the "fovea," the center of the retina at the back of the eye—then the fly remains constantly in the same retinal location.)

Let us call the set of changes in direction that results from a moving *vantage point* the "optic" flow field; it is purely ecological. By contrast, the set of changes that results from *eye movements* can be called the ocular, or "retinal," flow field; it is a set of changes in the eye.

Notice that, in these terms, an eye movement produces a retinal flow field that is often unlike an optic flow field. If the eye turns 10° to the right, *everything* on the retina moves by 10°; the distance to the elements is irrelevant. An object that was at the center of gaze is now 10° away from the center. What was 10° to the right of the center of gaze is now directly at the center of gaze. This *uniform* flow field can help distinguish, for instance, the effects of movement forward (which produce a flow field *radiating* out from the heading point) from the effects of eye rotations.

In nature, the two flow fields—one resulting from eye rotation and one from the movement of the vantage point—typically occur in combination. Indeed, if the observer rotates or moves his or her head, another component is added to the retinal flow field. The kind of motion the observer is undergoing is also a component (e.g., walking gives a different flow field than running does). Riding a horse, riding in a car, and riding in an airplane can give distinctive flow fields, too.

The passenger in the car fixating on a mark in the road can get a pronounced impression of one region where flow is slight and outward, left and right, while nearer regions of texture not only spread left and right but also rush outward from the center of gaze, like water welling over a waterfall and accelerating as it falls. Nevertheless, this impression is only centered on a mark on which the passenger happens to fixate. If the passenger makes a quick change of gaze to some other bump or pothole on this troubled road, the "waterfall" impression changes its location. Any waterfall impression that depends on where one happens to gaze is not a function of the environment or of the optic flow that tells us about the world. It is a function of the observer and tells the observer about the position and movement of the eyes.

Once again, vision involves a double impression in this. There is the momentary impression of a particular flow, visually, but also an impression of the directional flow that depends on observer motion. An important point in this is that, because retinal flow follows different *rules,* we can separate it, and therefore we can successfully respond to optical flow.

TEXTURES ACCRETING AND DELETING

Another pattern of texture change emphasized by Gibson involves "accretion" and "deletion" of texture. When an opaque object moves in front of a textured background, the leading edge of the object covers more and more of the background texture, while at the trailing edge, the background texture is being steadily uncovered at exactly the same rate (see Figure 2.4). From the observer's vantage point, the optic texture elements projected by the background are being "deleted" at the leading contour projected by the object. At the trailing contour of the object, the texture is "accreted."

The accretion and deletion of texture elements—*no matter* what those elements are—indicates that there is a moving object in the foreground, nearer to the vantage point than the surface whose elements are gradually appearing and disappearing, and it is so seen.

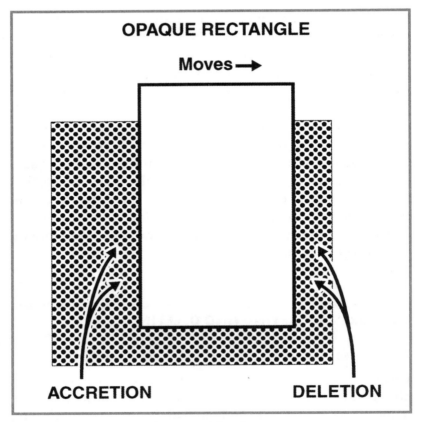

Figure 2.4. Accretion, Deletion, and Depth

However, this case is one in which the object and background are directly illuminated. In cases in which illumination comes from the side, the object often casts a deep shadow on the background. When the object moves, the shadow moves. The shadow can move over the background, and, at the contour of the shadow, accretion and deletion of a sort can occur. In this case, the deletion means that the shadow has reached the texture element, and the accretion means that illumination is reaching the texture element once again. *But* the shadow is seen as *flush* with the surface bearing the illumination, like a stain creeping along a surface. No part of the shadow literally covers the texture elements, and the shadow is *not* seen as being in the foreground, nearer to the observer's vantage point. It appears to be in the same plane as the texture. This may be because of the *systematic relationship* between the motion of the object and the motion of its shadow.

Accretion and deletion also occur when snow or rain falls and the observer is in a setting with a dark object in the distance. For example, my office at Scarborough College at the University of Toronto looks out across a tiled patio and the grassy slope of a ravine. Across the ravine is a dark mass of evergreen trees. In winter, the sky may be white, and the patio and grassy slope covered in snow. If there is snow gently falling, it is visible only when it is actually passing between the evergreens and the college. In effect, the snowflakes accrete optically at the upper contour of the evergreens. They delete at the lower border of the evergreens when their background is the snow-covered patio and slope.

Accretion and deletion provide an especially interesting instance of dual impressions in perception. The double nature of perception in this case lies in the impression that the elements that are going out of view are *going behind* something *or* losing illumination or visibility *but not* going out of existence *or* even being altered. They are perceived as continuing as they are, despite the fact that they can no longer be seen. *And* the observer has the impression that they continue to exist in more or less particular locations. (The secret in many conjuring tricks is that the object in question did *not* go to the location the audience fastens on!)

In contrast, if a dusty surface is wiped with a cloth, the cloth is seen as *taking up* the dust, just as a windshield wiper blade is seen as *removing* water drops. There is no dual impression—possibly because when the duster or the blade reverses direction, the dust and water drops do not accrete back into view. At any rate, the essential thing is that, in both sorts of cases—that of the snow scene and that of the windshield—our impressions are, *somehow, accurate.*

PICTURES

Perception's double character shows up in many aspects of vision. I believe it is likely to be one of the major factors that is constantly involved in picture perception and the difficulty that most people have in learning to draw. Often, we are aware of the elements in a scene and aware of amodal relations between the elements. When we try to draw, we must first solve the task of distinguishing the *visible* elements that give us particular impressions from the *amodal* relations that come from the elements. In addition, we must appreciate the angles and shapes subtended by the elements at our vantage point and how to reconstitute the same angles and shapes from picture surfaces viewed from particular vantage points. This is not child's play. Some of the key distinctions necessary for drawing can only be made with effort, ingenuity, and (typically) acquired skills for which we need instruction.

Figure 2.5 shows a drawing of a cube with a cross on it.[1] Are the lines in the cross at *acute* angles or at *right* angles to one another? We can have it both ways! Some lines on the *page* are at acute angles while, at the same time, on the *depicted cube* (i.e., in the pictured world), they are at right angles. We have to draw the lines on the page at one set of angles to give an impression of lines on a cube at another set of angles. What gives us the impression of right angles within the framework of a side of a cube can be seen as acute angles on the page. Perception can deal simultaneously with the two frameworks and get two impressions from one set of lines.[2]

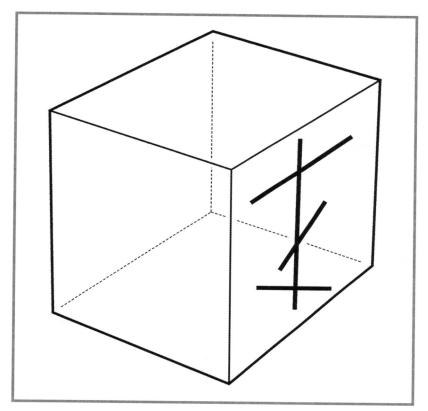

Figure 2.5. Which angles are right?

Adapted from *The Paridoxicon*, N. Falletta, Doubleday. Used with permission.

IN SUMMARY

To return to the wider everyday "real world," perception uses geometry. For example, it detects gradients and patterns of change in them. Invariants, such as the center of optical flow, can be detected within such gradients. Perception deals with relations, and these can give dual results, *but* these merely indicate what is a matter of an impression and what is in the environment. To me, the major point is that, even without the aid of cognition (see my "Further Look" in Chapter 8), we are fairly accurate at capturing the world because perception contains a fairly *smart geometry*, well related to optic information.

NOTES

1. Figure 2.5 was found in a fascinating collection by Nicholas Falletta: *The Paradoxicon.* (1983). New York: John Wiley.

2. There are other interesting cases in which there is a "bicameral" or "dual" or "double" fact in vision. For instance, in many patterns, we see subjective contours, but we can also tell that those contours are not actually present. For instance, Figure 2.6 below:

Figure 2.6. Dual Impression

Children of 4 or 5 years of age say "I see a line that isn't there." In some cases, the fact that the contour has no consistent brightness may be a telltale factor, providing a contradiction in perception that says, in effect, "Here lies error." At any rate, these bicameral or dual impressions indicate that perception has more than one center or "channel" operating at the same time. Impressions in one channel may not be present in another.

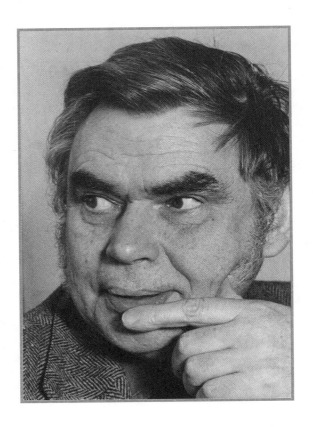

RICHARD L. GREGORY is well-known as the founder and editor of one of our most prestigious journals, *Perception,* which always includes his thought-provoking—and delightful—editorial. In addition, he has authored numerous articles and books on vision. One of the latter (*Eye and Brain,* 1966) has been so well received that it is the only psychology book to be recommended—among books on building log cabins and raising organic vegetables—in the original *Whole Earth Catalogue*! His title displays his British wit.

3

ACTION POTENTIALS TO POTENTIAL ACTIONS

RICHARD L. GREGORY

University of Bristol, England

This is how most of us now see perception: signals of electro-chemical action potentials from the senses, setting up perceptions that may initiate action. Unlike "knee-jerk" stimulus-response reflexes, perception is not stimulus driven. Perception allows behavior to be appropriate to knowledge of objects—appropriate even to unsensed characteristics. Thus, ice cream is *seen* to be cold; soap is recognized as uneatable, though useful in other ways. (You'd receive a nasty shock if soap were mistaken for ice cream; perception is not infallible.) This ability of eyes and brains to make rich use of limited and not directly relevant information suggests that perception is smart—making intelligent use of knowledge stored from the past.

Some theorists, however, believe that vision is achieved almost entirely "bottom-up" from sensory inputs. Others (including myself) hold that a large "top-down" contribution from stored knowledge is necessary for behavior to escape the tyranny of reflexes—to be appropriate to objects whatever the available stimuli. For that reason, the vast majority of human visual perception incorporates top-down knowledge selected from the past.

The exact proportion, however, is not important to me here. Suffice it to say that the most dramatic demonstration of the power of top-down knowledge is the *hollow mask:* A hollow mask of a face appears like a normal, nose-sticking-out face (see Figures 3.1a-3.1c)! Evidently, the perceptual hypothesis of a face is called up—is selected—by the mask from its nose and eyes and so on. This highly probable hypothesis contains the information that faces have their noses sticking out, not in. In fact, it requires full stereopsis (i.e., a very close look) to beat the top-down knowledge with bottom-up signals.

That knowledge can be so effective means that cognitive processes are extremely important. It also suggests that artificial intelligence (AI) seeing machines will not be effective without rich stores of readily available knowledge of objects and of themselves. For such a machine or organism to use its knowledge, it has to select appropriate analogies from the past to read the present situation. And there must always be possibilities of misreadings, especially in atypical situations when the selected past is inappropriate to the present. If selecting what is likely to be appropriate for seeing objects requires intelligence, it is appropriate to speak of the intelligent eye (Gregory, 1970).

If all problems are very largely solved by applying existing knowledge and known procedures, then only a small contribution of real-time processing is needed (cf. Gregory, 1987). If perception, too, is seen as problem solving—to guess what is out there—this fits the notion that the vision of humans and higher animals is very largely top-down, because top-down knowledge is the intelligence provided by previously solved problems. On this account, the eye/brain is intelligent. However (as for *all* intelligence), the massive contribution of stored knowledge may

Figure 3.1a. A "Hollow" Mask

dominate and swamp the much smaller contribution of the sort of intelligence required to select knowledge from the past to perceive the present for survival into the immediate future.

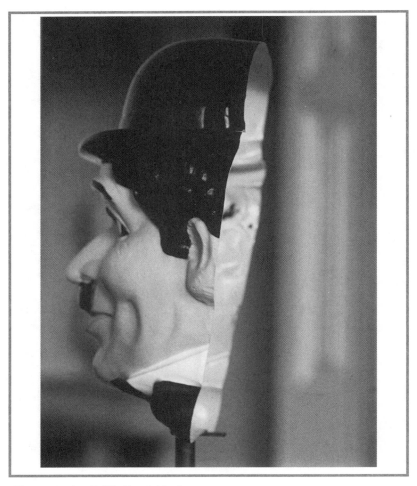

Figure 3.1b. A "Hollow" Mask

   This implies that, as well as the physiology involved, perception is an active, intelligent bunch of cognitive processes for generating hypotheses of the object world—*perceptual hypotheses*—which are the closest we ever get to physical reality apart from the predictive hypotheses of science, which often disagree with

Figure 3.1c. A "Hollow" Mask

appearances (Gregory, 1980). On this account, perceptions are essentially guesses of what might be out there, hypotheses mysteriously endowed with consciousness.

This is not, and certainly has not been, the only way of seeing perception. It is only fair to consider some of the alternatives.

ALTERNATIVE ACCOUNTS

This account of vision starts from the retinal *image,* which we know produces the neural signals of action potentials—which are all the brain ever receives. The discovery of action potentials had to wait for electronic technology early in the twentieth century.[1] This is hardly surprising. It is a strange fact, however, with rich implications for the history of philosophy and perception, that retinal images are quite a recent discovery. They were unknown to the Greeks, so Greek theories of vision, and much of their epistemology, look very odd to us now.

There were two primary accounts of imageless visual perception. One was that fingerlike rays shoot out of the eyes to touch objects. The other was that objects send out expanding "shells," like ripples spreading from a stone dropped in a pond but maintaining the forms of the objects; these surrogate surfaces of objects flow into the eyes to enter the mind. The first account was an analogy with touch, claiming that vision is as direct as touch contact. The main difficulty was that, when the eyes are opened, near and distant objects (including stars) appear together, but the rays were not supposed to shoot out of the eyes with infinite velocity. In the second account, a sensation (e.g., of red) is experienced directly with no intermediary steps from the surface of an object to our perception. The notion of expanding "shells" or "ripples" continued through the Middle Ages and became the sense data theory held by many recent philosophers (Broad, 1929). In its various forms, it promised direct experience and direct knowledge of the world of objects, but it came to be widely questioned with the realization of the physiological complexities of vision.

The astronomer and designer of telescopes, Johannes Kepler (1571-1630), was the first to detail the role of images in the eyes and how they are produced by geometrical optics. Why were they not discovered long before? Retinal images are but ghostly shades, scarcely of our world, and they are *not seen* as such. They are not seen because there are no eyes looking at them, which would lead to an endless regress of images—eyes-images-eyes-images—with no progress toward perception. The fact that they are never seen may explain why their existence remained unsuspected all through the history of philosophy and science until surprisingly recently, when images were produced by optical instruments and became familiar and well understood.

Kepler realized that, as objects are optically projected on the screen of the retina, they cannot be perceived at all directly or immediately, as the Greeks supposed. Yet despite Kepler's clear writing on this, the notion that vision involves merely "picking up" the world of objects continued in the thinking of the British empiricists of the eighteenth and nineteenth centuries.

The empiricist philosophers saw eyes as passive windows through which beauty and truth flood in, essentially without error. Perception just happened, without work or mental activity, and it provided secure premises for the philosophical belief in reality of objects. Now scientists are all too familiar with errors and ambiguities of data, so the notion of interpreting retinal images—"reading" from their signals the presence and nature of external objects—is familiar, and it is the start of all computational accounts of vision.

The eyes, ears, touch receptors, and so on detect patterns of stimuli from the external world, which are transmitted as action potential signals along afferent neural channels to be "read" by more-or-less cognitive "higher" processes. I shall suggest that these involve object knowledge and also general organizing rules (which may or may not be appropriate) for seeing objects. Much of this will be speculative but hopefully useful for present understanding and research into these important questions.

A great deal is known about photoreceptors (rods and cones); about the organization of receptive fields; about the transmission in nerves by discrete action potentials; and, especially–through the neurophysiological work of D. H. Hubel and T. N. Weisel (1968)–that specific features such as orientations and velocities and directions of motion are recognized by specifically tuned neural circuits. Spatial positions at the retina are soon lost in the cortical representations, which higher up are in specialized regions for processing movement, form, color, and so on. Curiously, it is *not* known how these visual projection areas, or processing modules (as many as 16 have been described), converge to form the final perception as a *unified* experience. The American philosopher Daniel C. Dennett (1991) suggests that they never do converge, perception being "multiple drafts," but it is not easy to see how parallel perceptions could lead to single decisions initiating behavior. Surely, the brain must make up its mind to be single-minded for decisions–except when we are thinking philosophically!

Biologically, the important point is that the eye's images are almost useless until they are read, or interpreted, in terms of objects–including *nonoptical* properties of objects. Reading the action potential signals from retinal images makes otherwise almost useless patterns of light in the eye highly significant. Because eyes provide "early warning"–probing distance without giving the game away–they are uniquely useful senses that gain time for planning. Eyes require and confer intelligence. No doubt, eyes have promoted many kinds of intelligence through the later stages of evolution.

BOTTOM-UP, TOP-DOWN, AND SIDE-WAYS

I have already introduced *bottom-up* signals–action potentials from the senses, especially from retinal images–and *top-down* information–stored knowledge of objects. There are also general organizing rules of perception, as emphasized early in the twentieth century by the Gestalt writers (see Ellis, 1938). It is possible that organizing rules are, to some extent, switched in as required for certain situations or tasks; for instance, there may be special rules for reading, while there are others for looking at pictures (though the rules are not always appropriate). I call all of these organizing rules *side-ways* rules, as an analogy with floppy disks for computers (though the brain may well be analog rather than digital). There is always a shortage of side-ways rules (like floppy disks!) to choose from. The general point here is that both top-down knowledge and side-ways rules can be inadequate and inappropriate, so errors and illusions can occur even though there is nothing wrong with the physiology.

What I am calling "side-ways" rules are not a historical paradigm for vision, but they can be referred back to the design of the first computer, to Charles Babbage's difference engine of the 1830s, with his insight that a gear-wheel computer must follow rules or algorithms. The gears cannot remain continuously linked if they are to accept results of other (unpredictable) computations, or data, as from internal look-up tables. Babbage disengaged his gear chains to allow what I am calling "side-ways" intervention. This is essential for any digital programmed computer—or any self-programming analog system such as a neural net—capable of a variety of tasks. Thus, there are the interesting neurological implications: Other regions and functions of the brain must *intervene* between top-down and bottom-up processing for *effective flexible perception*. These may be described as "side-ways."

It is important to note that, for higher animals, including humans, perception is not "driven" in a determined manner by either bottom-up signals or top-down knowledge. Strong evidence that it is not driven bottom-up is the phenomenon of spontaneous ambiguities in visual perception, as in E. G. Boring's famous "two women" drawing (see Figure 3.2). The point is, in such

Figure 3.2. One Picture, Two Women

cases, the same stimulus pattern can give rise to two or more very different alternative perceptions.[2] Furthermore, these are generally perceptions of likely objects. So there seem to be knowledge-based perceptual decision processes affected by likelihood. However, it is also clear that perception is not driven top-down from stored knowledge of objects; if it were, we would be unable to see anything unfamiliar. The fortunate fact is that we can see quite improbable things; otherwise, perceptual learning would be impossible.

This paradox of perception—choosing a likely alternative yet *not* being blind to the unlikely or even the impossible—may be resolved by seeing perception as following rules to generate what may be new hypotheses. There is a close link here to linguistics—to the fact that we can create and understand new sentences by following syntactical rules of grammar—yet it is easier to understand and express the familiar. The following of rules (from data and assumptions) is what allows hypotheses of science to transcend the given to create surprising novelty.

THE "INS" AND "OUTS" OF BLACK BOXES OF VISION

To explain vision and its rich phenomena, including illusions of many kinds, it is extremely important to reveal its physiology. This does not, however, imply that we will understand perception entirely from physiological knowledge, for we also need to know its *cognitive strategies*. If its stored knowledge, or a selected processing procedure, is not appropriate to a given situation, we may expect errors, even though there is nothing malfunctioning in the physiology. Thus, a calculator or a computer will give a wrong answer if set to carry out an inappropriate operation (e.g., if we press "add" instead of "multiply") even though there is no fault in its mechanism or its electronics. One would not discover the reason for the error in the "hardware"; rather, one must look at the "software" (us) for the explanation. This means that it can be useful to regard perception as an opaque black box, if we consider its ins and outs. This is the *psycho*logical approach. It is useful for directing the physiologists' attention to what may be discovered inside the black box, but it *also* may offer adequate explanations *even when* the physiology inside is entirely unknown.

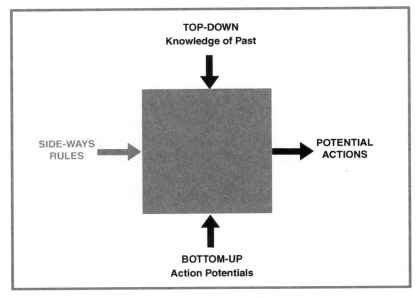

Figure 3.3. A Simple (but Incomplete) Model

A very simple black box diagram may represent bottom-up signals, top-down knowledge, and side-ways rules. Because this is only two-dimensional, I call it the flat box (see Figure 3.3).

However, it is clear—if only from the important fact that we can understand many phenomena of illusion *conceptually* but still be fooled *perceptually*—that top-down object knowledge does not encompass all we know or think we know. As Irv Rock already pointed out in Chapter 1, a disturbing feature of all visual illusion is that we can be deluded while knowing we are fooled. So, evidently, seeing and knowing are different.

But why should perceptions and conceptions be different? For one thing, the separation of perceptual from conceptual knowledge allows the experience of novelty to overcome the inertia of "wisdom." Furthermore, perception must work extremely *fast* for survival. One second of time is a long time perceptually, and thinking things out may take minutes, hours, days, even years! We may suppose it would simply take far too long to access our total store of knowledge; perception must find answers in a fraction of a second to be useful in real time. Thus, top-down for perception must be from a *restricted* knowledge base.

And there are inadequate checks, one upon the others. Conflicts with conceptual knowledge (e.g., being fooled perceptually by illusions we know and understand conceptually) can remain unresolved for years–for a lifetime. Instead, the black box of visual processing is *fed* conceptual knowledge *slowly;* in turn, it is *slowly,* and sometimes not at all, *affected by* conceptual knowledge. No doubt, perceptual learning and learning from perception are slow, for accepting significant new knowledge requires a great deal of reorganization in the "spread sheet" of the mind. And, for such inductions, just a few instances are dangerous. Thus, the system *must* be slow–just as science is slow–to build *reliable* generalizations for predictive knowledge. At any rate, we should amend Figure 3.3 with an extra "box" for conceptual knowledge largely separate from perceptual object knowledge, each feeding the other, slowly and seemingly inefficiently (see Figure 3.4).

I have warned that this account may look speculative. Let's look at some suggestive data, especially phenomena of visual illusions.

DISTORTIONS FROM INAPPROPRIATE KNOWLEDGE AND RULES

To show that top-down knowledge can affect bottom-up signals, we may consider the *size-weight illusion.* Small objects, when lifted, feel heavier than larger objects of the same actual weight. Since larger objects are generally heavier than smaller objects,

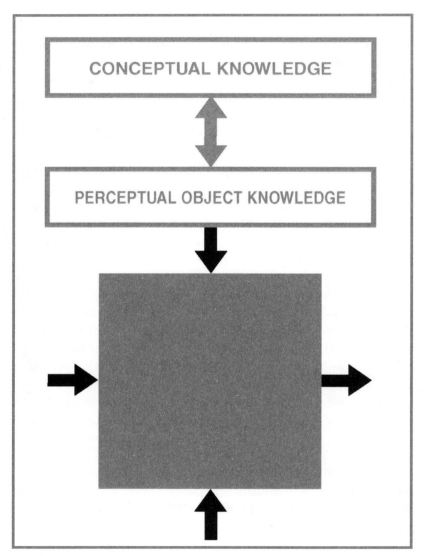

Figure 3.4. Separating *Kinds* of Knowledge

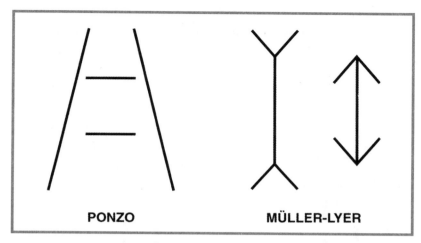

Figure 3.5. Two Classic Illusions of Size

the smaller object sets up less muscle power for lifting, and so it seems surprisingly heavy. This must be based on our knowledge that larger things are generally heavier; the illusion occurs when this knowledge does not apply.

The essential notion here is that many phenomena of illusion, especially distortions of size or distance, can be generated by inappropriately applied knowledge or rules. The point is that these are top-down and side-ways illusions that can be essentially explained *without* looking into the black box—that is, without reference to the physiology. Examples of side-ways rules generating systematic measurable errors are the size distortions that can occur when distance is *represented* but not actually present (e.g., in flat pictures containing perspective). This is the start of an explanation for many of the classical distortion illusions such as the Ponzo and the Müller-Lyer (see Figure 3.5).

The upper horizontal line of the Ponzo figure is signaled, by perspective, as being more distant. It looks longer than the same-sized lower line because, in a real sense, if it were farther, it

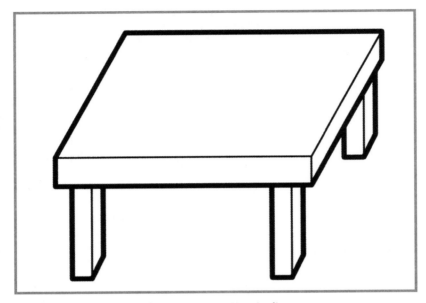

Figure 3.6. The Harm of Inappropriate Size Scaling

would give a smaller retinal image; however, it would be expanded by what we call perceptual "size scaling" to look much the same size as a nearer line of the same length. The notion is that, in the Ponzo illusion figure, the normally appropriate size scaling is set by the typical depth cues even when depth is not consciously seen. The Müller-Lyer illusion is similar, being perspective drawings of wall corners pointed away or at you, respectively. Again, the more distant-signaled line is expanded.

Similar distortions can occur top-down from assumed, though not explicitly signaled, depth (as in Figure 3.6).

In this figure, the upper edge (assumed to be distant) appears longer than the lower; the sides do not look quite parallel, but they are. In this case, top-down knowledge of tables has set size scaling appropriately for an actual table but inappropriately for a flat picture, and the picture appears distorted (while a truly three-dimensional table would look rectangular). Again, the notion is that cues to distance set size scaling for a more distant object or feature, but, since the picture is flat, this is inappropriate, producing expansion where nonexisting distance is (wrongly) signaled.

What is especially relevant about this "inappropriate size scaling" theory of distortion illusions is that it is a *psychological* rather than a *physiological* explanation. Certainly, one can go on to ask, for example, how size scaling is triggered and how it works physiologically. This is to look inside the black box. The point here is that some explanations (psychological) are essentially in terms of the ins and outs of the box and are useful even though the physiology is not well known.

BEYOND THE FLAT BOX

So far, we have three orthogonal dimensions of processing: bottom-up, top-down, and side-ways. The first provides real-time data from sensory signals. The second provides stored knowledge for "reading" the data, making use of various subtle cues (general and object-specific) for interpreting sensory data, including those from retinal images. The third (side-ways) includes various interventions—no doubt at many levels—between bottom-up and top-down so that perception is not *driven* by either current data or stored knowledge alone. These interventions may be algorithms, attentional selection, commands (e.g., to try alternatives to reach possible better solutions, as in spontaneous changes seen in Figure 3.2), and so on.

Is there a third dimension for the black box? Surely, there is. Perception is not just for admiring scenes—it is for controlling behavior with respect to the task at hand. It must send advice, ultimately commands, to motor behavior. Our third dimension involves such input—specifying the task, hence attention and "set"—

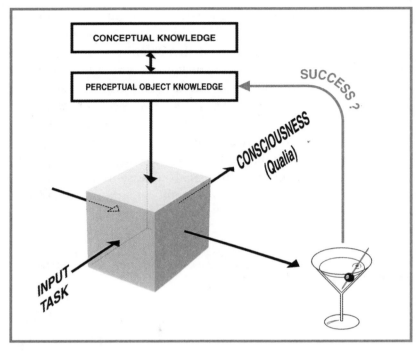

Figure 3.7. The Complete Model

and output to consciousness. (Then there is feedback, for learning from behavioral successes and failures.) Most mysterious is consciousness. This scheme is shown in Figure 3.7, in which we see that an *input* task may select *side-ways* rules to apply to bottom-up signals. Successes and failures of *output* (here, balancing a glass) feed back to correct perceptual (and conceptual) knowledge.

Consciousness

The mystery of consciousness is *why* we have sensations, or "qualia"—such as sensations of red or of pain—and *what,* if anything, *they do*. Here are a few thoughts in terms of the black box scheme.

Bottom-up information is of the present; top-down information and side-ways rules are carried with us and used to predict and control the future. When one opens one's eyes, immediately there are visual qualia. When the eyes are shut, the qualia disappear, to be replaced by shadowy, surprisingly inaccurate, memory.[3] Possibly, this is less so for painters; for the rest of us, the qualia soon fade to insignificance. So we might think of qualia as *tagging the present*. The "now" is uniquely important for decisions of action.

Qualia seem most intense when there is surprise. Surprise is closely related to the amount of (probably useful) information. Thus, very familiar objects (e.g., pictures on one's own walls) are virtually invisible unless attention is paid to them, and they are not very useful most of the time.

Qualia *seem* to come from bottom-up signals rather than from top-down knowledge or side-ways rules. Qualia can, however, be affected by changes top-down. For example, Ernst Mach's (1959, p. 209) "slipping corner" changes brightness according to whether the dark region is accepted as a shadow or as marks (or a stain or paint or whatever) on the surface (see Figure 3.8).

Thus, we begin to see different kinds of perceptual phenomena that, because they appear as deviations from the physical world, we call illusions. Because classifications are very important in science, it is worth trying to classify illusions in terms of appearances and causes. The parallel with errors of language that emerges is suggestive, for both language and perception are *descriptions*. The **kinds** of visual illusion seem to fall naturally into four classes: *ambiguities* (e.g., the "two women" figure); *distortions* (e.g., Ponzo and Müller-Lyer figures); *paradoxes* (e.g., the "impossible objects" mentioned by Irv Rock); and *fictions* (e.g., Gaetano Kanizsa's illusory contours). The primary **causes** seem to fall into the following categories: *physical* (mirrors, mirages, etc.);

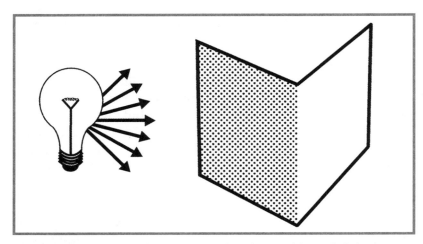

Figure 3.8. Try seeing this as a creased card viewed from slightly above with the corner toward you and then as viewed from below with the corner away from you. When the card reverses in depth, the dark region may change in lightness according to whether it is seen as a "shadow" (corner sticking in) or as "something" on the surface (corner sticking out). As a shadow, it appears light, no doubt because shadows, not being objects that can be handled, are largely ignored. At any rate, the point is that the change must be top-down because there is no change in the bottom-up (retinal) signals. (This works far better if an actual bent card with a true shadow is used. It is well worth trying out!)

physiological (e.g., signal distortions resulting from interactions between retinal cells, adaptation, and afterimages); and *cognitive* (by both misapplied knowledge such as in the hollow face and misapplied rules such as perspective in the Ponzo and Müller-Lyer illusions; cf. Gregory, 1994).

THE PRESENT AND FUTURE

Speculating about and experimenting with the "ins" and "outs" only take us so far. But at least they should be useful for suggesting where to look at physiological data from. In fact, although beyond the present *main* purposes, a strong case can be made (see my "Further Look" in Chapter 9) that physiological and cognitive research are already—and *at last*—converging to throw much-needed light into the black box.

NOTES

1. From hints going back to Galvani and Volta, Keith Lucas and E. D. Adrian discovered the pulses of electricity in nerve just before the 1914-1919 World War. Keith Lucas died in an air crash in 1916. Adrian became Lord Adrian, Master of Trinity College, Cambridge. (See E. D. Adrian, 1928, *The basis of sensation*. London: Christophers.)

2. What *initiates* such switches between possibilities, giving often very different alternative perceptions of the same picture or object? William James (1890) and Sir Karl Popper and Sir John Eccles (1977) have suggested that, although the *brain* is entirely responsible for creating perceptions from stimulus patterns, the *mind* intervenes on occasions to switch perceptions. William James discusses this notion critically, but Popper and Eccles (who do not refer to James) make this their strongest argument for saying that the mind is separate from the brain yet is a causal agent affecting the brain. On the other hand, the vast majority of brain scientists deny a mind-brain duality, holding that the mind is somehow generated by brain function. Then we may simply say that some other brain process initiates the switching. This avoids the metaphysics of a separate mind playing on the synapses of the brain as a (ghostly) pianist plays on the keys of a piano.

3. It is extremely interesting to shut your eyes and try to describe (or to look away and draw) what you have just been seeing. The inaccuracies are humbling.

PART II

Their "Audience"

As we have seen, a gratifying degree of agreement has emerged that vision is in some sense, at some times, intelligent. But consensus is only the weakest sort of evidence. What would others say of their thoughts? And what about the *differences* among our authors?

ULRIC NEISSER of Cornell University is one of *the* central figures in the birth of cognition psychology. Back in the 1960s, a number of people were working on specific lines of research that were to define the core of this new field, but it was he who put all their efforts together in what is undoubtedly the first major book on the subject and gave the field its name: *Cognitive Psychology* (1967). The old behavioristic "experimental psychology" didn't have a chance after that.

4

ADMIRABLY ADAPTIVE, OCCASIONALLY INTELLIGENT

ULRIC NEISSER

Cornell University

The chief reason why Irvin Rock and Richard Gregory want to call vision intelligent is probably because they admire it so much: "Intelligent" is a compliment. (I think this is the chief reason because—as we shall see—their other arguments aren't strong.) So let me say right up front that I, too, am an admirer of vision. What I find most admirable, however, is not its so-called intelligence but the sheer fact that it works so well, that people see the world around them pretty much as it is. They do not do this by means of subtle inference or clever reasoning but simply by picking up the appropriate optical information. Although something like intelligence may be relevant to vision in one special case—the case of picture perception, with its dual awareness of picture and depicted scene—it is a mistake to generalize from seeing pictures to seeing the real environment.

The most obvious problem with describing vision as "intelligent" is that it often seems so dumb. My colleagues are fully aware of this problem, although for some reason it does not weaken their convictions. Here are some of Irv Rock's own examples of the stupidity of vision:

- We can't help seeing an oddly long horse in his partially occluded drawing even though we know that no such horses exist and the figure itself includes many others of normal shape.
- We persist in seeing the subjective contours of the Kaniza triangle even though we are perfectly aware that there are not such lines on the page.
- We continue to see distortions of size and length in classical illusions such as the Ponzo even after we have measured the lines in question many times.
- We see real human beings undergo changes of size as they walk around in the Ames room, although we know this cannot possibly happen.

If perception does depend on inference, the homunculus who does the inferring must be a dumbculus indeed! But if it does not use inference, what do such demonstrations actually show? I think they show that perception depends on the available stimulus information, nothing more. Sometimes the relevant information is local; as Irvin Rock says, "What is present in a given local region will exert a powerful effect on how that region and regions next to it are perceived." In other setups, it is more global; the perspective lines visible in the Ames room govern perception of the whole layout. Either way, the processing seems to be entirely bottom-up, unaffected by knowledge of the world. There are infinitely many such cases, most of which produce veridical perception rather than error.

Given these demonstrations, how does Irv Rock justify his belief that vision is "intelligent"? Essentially, by suggesting causal stories in which something like inference plays a part. In the Ames room, for example, he says that "It is a 'plausible' assumption on the part of the brain that the rear wall is in a place perpendicular to the line of sight." Maybe so, but a plausible assumption on my part is that no such assuming is necessary. What we see in the Ames room depends—like most visual experience—on the optic array at the point of observation. Ames rooms are constructed so that the array visible at the peephole *specifies* an (illusory) rectangular layout, so we see just that. (Incidentally, all the Ames illusions depend on limiting observation to a single, carefully positioned peephole; normal head movements would reveal the real layout instantly.)

Irvin Rock's interpretation of apparent ("stroboscopic") motion seems even more romantic. He writes as if seeing motion in stroboscopic displays were an intellectual success: "The brain is faced with an unusual problem . . . [to which] perceiving a single object *moving* is a good solution." But crabs and flies respond to such displays just as we do; are they solving intellectual problems too? Luckily, there is a simpler interpretation. Rather than being the solution to a problem, apparent motion results from a simple failure of discrimination. Within certain limits, the motion detectors of the eye just can't tell the difference between a rapid succession of stimuli and a genuinely continuous motion. Why should they? There were no stroboscopic displays in the evolutionary past of the visual system and, hence, no selective pressure to make that distinction.

Richard Gregory's arguments for the intelligence of vision are perhaps more complex. He particularly stresses the phenomenon of the hollow mask; really a hollowed-out concave shape, the mask is seen as a "normal, nose-sticking-out face." This illusion is said to be "the most dramatic demonstration of the power of top-down knowledge." Dramatic it may be indeed, but generalizable it is not. Neuroscientists now generally agree that seeing faces represents a distinct and unique form of perception—one based on special, innately prepared neural mechanisms. Human beings respond to facelike patterns with unusual interest from earliest infancy, and they continue to do so throughout life. Faces seem to look out at us from random textures, from passing clouds, from dappled shadows in the woods (that is why we are so ready to believe in forest gods and spirits), from all kinds of haphazard patterns where no real face exists. On the other side, there is the clinical syndrome known as *prosopagnosia,* in which patients lose the ability to recognize faces but (in some cases) lose almost nothing else. Because face perception is a special case, the example of the hollow mask cannot be used to argue for any general preeminence of "top-down" mechanisms.

Some of the arguments advanced for the intelligence of perception are interestingly inconsistent. In the case of the hollow mask, vision is said to be intelligent because preexisting knowledge (the face schema) overrides present stimulus information (about the relative depth of the features of the mask). In the case of the Ames room, vision is said to be intelligent for just the opposite reason: Preexisting knowledge (that people don't change sizes as they walk) does not override present stimulus information (at the peephole). In my view, neither example has anything at all to do with intelligence. The first just illustrates our readiness to see faces; the other shows the importance of perspective structure for seeing the layout of environmental surfaces.

Much of Richard Gregory's chapter expounds his own metaphorical model of vision, a model that includes "top-down," "bottom-up," and "side-ways" processes as well as "qualia" and other mysterious matters. I have been criticizing models of this general sort for some 20 years but will resist the temptation to do so here (Neisser, 1976). There's no need to beat this particular horse any longer: It's quite dead. The modern neuroscience of vision, still in a rudimentary stage of development, has already revealed structures that are far too complex for the old models and metaphors to accommodate. It is my guess that a system that treats "where" and "what" as separate problems, that occupies about half the primate brain and includes more than two dozen distinct spatial mappings, is not going to be easily characterized by any flowchart.

Perhaps the best argument *for* the role of intelligence in vision derives from picture perception. (Richard Gregory does not make this argument as explicitly as John Kennedy does, but his account of the optical illusions relies on it nevertheless.) J. J. Gibson (1979) pointed out two decades ago that viewing pictures requires a kind of dual perception. A picture is a surface and can be seen as such, but it also presents some of the information that the depicted scene itself would present if it were actually at hand. Picking up both kinds of information and using them independently, we see the picture as a thing in its own right (perhaps it is a painted piece of canvas stretched over a frame) as well as the virtual scene that it depicts. This is quite a trick, and it apparently takes quite a lot of brain. There is no serious evidence that any animal other than Homo sapiens can manage it. What's more, it serves purposes other than the immediate control of action. For all these reasons, it may make sense to say that viewing pictures involves a kind of intelligence, although direct perception of the environment does not. But even here the mark of intelligence is not the use of "inference"; it is the ability to subdivide a richly overlapping complex of information and respond selectively to its parts.

Richard Gregory's account of the optical illusions explains most of them as by-products of picture perception. The Ponzo illusion, for example, is a picture in which—at least to some extent—the converging "railroad tracks" are seen as specifying three-dimensional depth. This, in turn, affects the perceived lengths of the horizontal lines, because to some extent they are seen as being at different depths in virtual space. If this theory is right, such illusions can indeed be regarded as by-products of pictorial vision. Nevertheless, psychologists concerned with picture perception—and a fortiori those concerned with perception of the real environment—would be well advised to leave them alone. I would argue that, still mysterious after a century of study, simple line-pattern illusions have never provided the slightest insight into *more significant* modes of perception. My own interest does not lie in the study of illusion but in the smoothly adapted mechanisms of ordinary vision and the information they pick up.

What is that information? Fortunately for the reader of this volume, John Kennedy devotes much of his chapter to three important types (all of which are drawn from the work of J. J.

Gibson): (a) texture gradients that provide information about the ground on which we walk, or might walk; (b) optic flow that specifies the layout of objects on that ground as well as our own path of movement; and (c) occlusion and disocclusion (specified by the deletion/accretion of texture elements), which indicate the relative positions of objects with respect to ourselves. I do not know whether John Kennedy regards the visual system's use of these invariants as "intelligent"; for me, they are just adaptation at its best.

I conclude these comments by addressing one other classic question—a question that will introduce a rather different perspective on vision as a whole. How do we manage to recognize and categorize objects (i.e., to see what things are)? One way to address this problem is to invoke concepts that have been effective in other areas of perception. Thus, John Kennedy, knowing that certain specific patterns (textures, flow fields, etc.) specify where things are, proposes that there may be equally specific patterns for object identity. Here he follows Gibson, who also believed that every object and every category of objects had its own "invariant." But there are several reasons to think that this view is quite mistaken. Perceiving *what* is very different from perceiving *where*.

First of all, no one has ever been able to define the invariants that might specify the visually identifiable categories of everyday life such as *car, bird, President Lincoln,* and *my old sweater.* This failure to find "category invariants" contrasts with the successful discovery of invariants for layout: particular optical patterns that specify given surface orientations, object positions, and directions of motion. It may be that objects are not identified on the basis of invariant patterns at all but by accumulating motley arrays of evidence from various sources. This is true for basic-level categories such as *car* and *bird* as well as for individual categories such as *President Lincoln* or *my old sweater.*

Second, we are often mistaken about what we see. Object identification is easily influenced by motives, expectations, plausible reasoning, and the like. This is not the case for seeing where things are; perception of layout seems entirely independent of such biases. It is also noteworthy that a preliminary object identification is often overturned by later-coming information; looking more closely, I see that it's not Lincoln, not my old sweater after all. Under normal conditions, such reversals do not occur in perceiving the layout of the environment.

Finally, it has been known since the work of Ungergleider and Mishkin (1982) that the machinery of vision includes two anatomically distinct cortical subsystems, one for perceiving *what* (identifying objects and categories) and the other for perceiving *where* (locating objects and acting on them). These subsystems are dissociated in some clinical neurological syndromes and can be lesioned separately in experimental animals. A monkey with damage to the "what" subsystem is rather like a human agnosic, unable to identify even very familiar patterns. In contrast, a monkey with damage to the "where" subsystem cannot reach and grasp the things it sees.

In summary, two distinct subsystems may be involved in normal ambient vision. The where system relies on specific invariants that specify layout and position and movement; several such invariants are described in Kennedy's chapter. The what system works in a less geometrically organized way, accumulating evidence rather than detecting specific critical patterns. Does it make sense to call either system "intelligent"? I think not. Each of them just chugs along, doing what it does. Only in the special case of picture perception, where both systems seem to operate in a uniquely human dual mode, does the use of that term make sense to me. But while ambient vision may not be *intelligent,* it is certainly *admirable,* keeping us richly and reliably aware of the environmental situation in which we find ourselves. Who would ask for more?

ROSS H. DAY of LaTrobe University in Australia has been called the "father of empirical psychology" of that continent. But more important to my (perhaps provincial) mind is his prodigious discoveries of new, usually visual, phenomena. And more admirable still is his tenacious insistence in all of these innumerable cases not only to report an effect but also to dissect it and analyze it to achieve and test an *understanding* of the case at hand. His is truly an inspirational career.

5

LAUREL AND HARDY AND ME

ROSS H. DAY

La Trobe University, Australia

THREE THEORIES OF HUMAN PERCEPTION

I shall begin this commentary by recounting an early perceptual experience that both intrigued and troubled me as a child. I was greatly addicted (and still am) to the movies of Stan Laurel and Oliver Hardy. Among my favorites was *Brats,* made in 1930, which I saw when I was about 8. In it, Stan and Oliver were each blessed with a son who bore an extraordinarily close resemblance to his father, so much so that I knew I was being tricked but could not fathom how. It was some time before I had a flash of insight: Stan Laurel and Oliver Hardy, whose deceptive size was aided and abetted by boys' clothes, went through their (to me) screamingly funny routines on a greatly enlarged set. The rooms, a well-remembered mantelshelf, a fireplace, and a chair in which they sat were all greatly enlarged. The chair scene is shown in Figure 5.1.

Figure 5.1. Stan Laurel and Oliver Hardy

My reason for drawing attention to this early experience is to make a general point about the three accounts of perception set out here by Irvin Rock, John Kennedy, and Richard Gregory. I suspect that if a curious child after watching *Brats* were to ask each of these contributors, "Why do Laurel and Hardy look so small?" he or she would be given three different answers.

Irvin Rock would reply, as he has done in his account of the Ames room, that the reduction in the apparent size of the two men is the outcome of an "intelligent" perceptual system. Even though we know that there is a trick and that the two men are not really smaller, an autonomous system insulated from knowledge and following its own laws construes the scene in terms of small individuals in a rather large chair. What those laws are in this case are not entirely clear to me. The only perceptual law that occurs to me as a basis for this very persistent illusion is that, when objects or individuals are contained in another—in this situation, a chair—the rules of the perceptual system dictate that what is contained must be smaller than the container. That is, in the absence of other *references* for size, the individuals in the chair appear smaller and the chair itself larger, contrary to our acquired knowledge about the relative sizes of persons and chairs. I shall return to this point in the final section of this commentary and consider the role of stimulus references in the ways things look to us.

If John Kennedy were asked why Stan Laurel and Oliver Hardy look so small, contrary to our acquired knowledge about the size of well-known adult actors, I presume he would reply in terms of the information available in the total stimulus array. He would not invoke an "intelligent" rule-following process but argue, as J. J. Gibson presumably also would have done, that the answer lies in the complex pattern of stimulation. The percept of the reduced size of two people in a big chair represents the response of the visual system to a distinctive, detailed pattern. In other words, the question would most likely be answered in terms of the proximal stimulus pattern that, by itself, and without recourse to an intelligent process of past experience, specifies small individuals in a large chair. However, what particular higher-order variables in the stimulus array specify these relative sizes is unclear.

Richard Gregory states that "perception is not stimulus driven. Perception allows behavior to be appropriate to knowledge of objects." And he adds that "Perception is smart—making intelligent use of knowledge stored from the past." In these terms, it is difficult to understand why Stan Laurel and Oliver Hardy are seen as small—unless, of course, it is the children's clothes they are wearing. However, even young boys, their resemblance to two well-known actors notwithstanding, would occupy more of a standard armchair than they do in Figure 5.1. Somehow, top-down processing based on knowledge about people and chairs seems to have failed in this situation and conveyed the strong impression of small figures. Somehow the stimulus has prevailed over knowledge acquired from past experience.

The different answers to the question "Why do Laurel and Hardy look so small?" each derived from a different view of the nature and processes of human perception, are at the same time both worrying and challenging. They are worrying because they cannot all be right and challenging because there has to be a right answer based on a principle or principles that account also for all of the phenomena to which the three "key-note" contributors have drawn our attention.

I do not believe that the differences between the three theories of perception proposed by Irvin Rock, John Kennedy, and Richard Gregory are simply a matter of semantics (i.e., different terms that obscure essential similarities between the three arguments). The differences are profound and deeply rooted in the history of psychology. Irvin Rock stresses the insulation of perception from experience-gained knowledge, emphasizing a notion of a perceptual "intelligence" that is lawful. John Kennedy stresses the primary role of the proximal pattern of light that contains all the subtle information necessary to perceive the external state of affairs. He emphasizes a system that has evolved to make use of these higher-order, subtle properties of the proximal stimulus array. Richard Gregory's view of perception is very much based on unconscious inference, emphasizing the inadequacies of the stimulus pattern and the role of knowledge in lending meaning to it.

A commentator is therefore faced with the problem of either reconciling these seemingly irreconcilable differences or suggesting another approach to a general explanation of the now very large body of veridical and illusory phenomena with which textbook and reference works on human perception are replete. I do not feel that the former course is realizable and therefore propose to take the latter.

THE EVOLUTIONARY ORIGIN
OF HUMAN PERCEPTION

Before turning to the key issue of an explanation of human perception and to the key question of this book—whether "intelligence" is in some sense involved—it is relevant first to consider two matters: the evolution of perception and the environments in which it probably occurred.

Perceptual capacities and their modification with experience can reasonably be regarded as products of environmental pressures and biological responses to those pressures such that the probability of survival and reproduction of the species is enhanced. Although this view is implicit in numerous treatises on human perception, it is seldom emphasized. However, John Kennedy hints at the evolutionary origins of perception when he states, "In nature, a certain pattern indicates a tree (or a wolf or a river). . . . Sensory patterns are distinctive, and they specify particular sources in the environment of the observers." Thus, our capacity to perceive objects at a distance as more or less the same size even though their image sizes vary and as more or less the same shape, with changes in their retinal shape consequent on their orientation to the observer, can be regarded as an evolved capacity. To see things the way they are clearly has adaptive and survival advantages.

Because most experimental work on perception has been (and continues to be) conducted in laboratories, often with constraints imposed on the observer, we tend to overlook that it evolved in response to the pressures imposed in response to environments radically different from those in which it is traditionally investigated. It can be presumed that these environments were largely "unbuilt," without neatly laid-out roads, rectangular buildings, or carpentered furnishings. They consisted of crude paths, plains, scrub, forests, hills, mountains, rocks, and other natural formations. Furthermore, these environments were three-dimensional, with land (or sea) and sky separated by straight or irregular horizons and with a ubiquitous gravitational force. It is often useful and salutary to bear in mind the sorts of environments in which human and infrahuman perception has evolved in the interest of adaptation and survival. It is particularly useful to do so when we are tempted to interpret perceptual phenomena in terms of constructed or "carpentered" spaces or objects.

THE REFERENTIAL BASIS OF PERCEPTION

Given that the three accounts of perception proposed by Irvin Rock, John Kennedy, and Richard Gregory are markedly different, the question arises as to whether there is another, more comprehensive theory that can account for the highly diverse phenomena to which these contributors and I have drawn attention. I believe there is, and I shall now attempt to sketch it without going into too much detail.

The essence of the proposal is that the visual perceptual system has evolved to render ambiguous, often progressively exposed, and frequently fragmented proximal stimuli unequivocal and unified. This "disambiguation" and unification is achieved by references to other features in the total stimulus array. These references have a good deal in common with what have traditionally, and I think misleadingly, been called "cues." The term *reference* to describe these features and *referencing* to describe the perceptual process to which they give rise are preferred because they better capture what I believe to be the basis of visual perception; the term *cue* carries with it an implication of a signal or reminder, as when actors or singers forget their lines. On the other hand, the term *reference* also has a good deal in common with J. J. Gibson's higher-order variables and stimulus correlates, although Gibson does not incorporate the idea of a referencing *process*.

Let me introduce these ideas via the Ames room effect. A photograph of this room taken from the carefully positioned viewing aperture shows a rectangular room with the walls at right angles to the floor and ceiling and the far wall rectangular and at right angles to the axis of the lens. This is much how the room appears to an observer viewing it with one eye at the aperture. The close similarity between what the camera "sees" and what the observer sees emphasizes that the projection of the room at the retina is that of a regularly shaped room. The reason that the room is mistakenly seen this way rather than as a very irregular three-dimensional space is that two key references for the distances of the far corners—those of retinal disparity (which depends on viewing with both eyes) and monocular parallax (which depends on head movement)—are eliminated. In other words, without reference to depth, the projected image of a rectangular room prevails.

In the three forms of the Ponzo figure in the left-hand panel of Figure 5.2, two horizontal lines of the same length lie within the boundaries of a relatively large or small space and so occupy a small or large part of the space, respectively. I suggest that the amount of space occupied by an element is a reference for the apparent size of the element. If the element occupies a small area of the delineated field, it appears smaller than an identical element occupying a large area.

There is a key and, as will be argued, important difference between the Ponzo illusions and the Müller-Lyer illusions (versions of which are shown in the right-hand panel of Figure 5.2). In the former, observers are asked to compare the lengths of the two line elements within the frames; in the latter, they are asked to compare the lengths of two intrinsic features, the spaces between the two terminal elements. In the Ponzo figure, the two lines are separate, lying in a bounded area. In the Müller-Lyer figure, the

Figure 5.2. Variations on Two Classic Illusions

two component spaces are an intrinsic feature of the figure and inseparable from it. It is proposed that, whereas in the Ponzo figure, the size of the enclosing field is the reference for apparent length, in the Müller-Lyer figure, the reference is the overall length of the figure itself. In these terms, the size of the figure or object is the reference of an intrinsic component. This point is brought out very clearly in Figure 5.3, in which the horizontal extents of the rectangle, oval, and diamond are exactly the same.

There is one further point that is worth making in the context of this discussion of the references for size. Several years ago, a book was published (Hershenson, 1989) devoted entirely to the moon illusion: the greater apparent size of the full moon when it

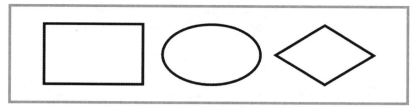

Figure 5.3. Another Size Illusion

is just above the horizon than when it is high in the sky. It included some 19 papers and an annotated bibliography of nearly 300 papers published between 322 B.C. and 1988 A.D.! Maurice Hershenson, the editor, stated in his concluding summary of the contributions,

> Is the moon illusion an illusion of perceived size or is it also an illusion of perceived distance? Historically, there has been little agreement on this point. Has the situation been changed by the opportunity afforded by this volume to re-examine the problem? The answer is a clear and resounding "No!" (p. 377)

It is, of course, rather disappointing to find that, after about 2,300 years of scholarly debate, we still cannot explain a perceptual phenomenon that occurs a dozen times a year every year. In terms of the referential theory that I am proposing here, the apparent size of the moon is likely to be a matter of the references for size in the visual stimulus array. From this standpoint, it is possible—and perhaps crassly brave—to make a suggestion as to what this reference might be: A figure or pattern in a clearly bounded area such as a sheet of paper appears larger than the same figure cut out and viewed from the same distance. Is it possible that the greater size of the horizon moon is the result of the reference provided by the bounded terrain between observer and horizon, and the smaller size of the zenith moon is the absence of any such bounded region in the open sky? This is not a new idea; Luhr suggested it in 1898. It is certainly worth trying with artificial "moons" in bounded and unbounded visual fields.

IS PERCEPTUAL REFERENCING AN INTELLIGENT PROCESS?

Where do these considerations leave us in regard to whether or not the visual perceptual system is an "intelligent" one? That is to say, whether it follows rules so that an "intelligent" solution to a perceptual "problem" is achieved. My own approach to this issue, the issue with which this book is largely concerned, is one of caution. To begin with, the term *intelligent* carries numerous meanings, so in applying it to perception, we must be quite clear as to which of those meanings we have in mind. This is not to split hairs; to state that perception is intelligent in the sense of learning from experience is thoroughly supported by a considerable body of data. We learn to discriminate between fine differences in stimulus properties, and we learn to recognize particular faces, words, and signs. However, to state that perception is intelligent in the sense of responding successfully to a new experience is by no means supported by experimental data. To respond to the pairs of equal-spaced Müller-Lyer figures in Figure 5.2 as if they are different in size could hardly be regarded as successful. Responding to the horizontal extents of the three figures in Figure 5.3 as if they are different also cannot be regarded as intelligent in this sense.

To avoid confusion, I prefer to concentrate on the established properties of perception revealed by well over a century of experimental inquiry. If we accept that human vision is, as in other species, a biological system that has evolved primarily in the interests of adaptation, survival, and procreation, it seems to me sufficient to establish its operating principles unclouded by reference to "intelligence." For example, if, as argued here, veridical perception of exterior and interior three-dimensional shape derives from specifiable reference in the proximal stimulus array, it follows that perception will vary as those references are systematically varied. If they are reduced or eliminated, the perceived shape reverts to that of its retinal image, and if they are present, the shape approximates its physical dimensions. To me, it is redundant to regard the outcomes of reference manipulations as intelligent. Likewise, if the overall size of an object is a reference for the perceived size of its internal spaces, then manipulation of the latter will result in a variation in the former—hence the Müller-Lyer and other illusions. Again, it seems unnecessary to treat this reference-determined outcome as an "intelligent" solution to a perceptual problem. It is simply the way perception operates given the references that are available.

THEODORE E. PARKS

And now, in the interest of "full disclosure," I must finally introduce myself. For as long as I've been interested in vision, I have
particularly enjoyed explanations that emphasized inferential
"perceptual hypothesis," as promoted over the years by Irvin
Rock, Richard L. Gregory, and, originally, von Helmholtz (although we do not all share his insistence that these inferences are
all based on learning). Having said that, however, what could
someone like me–or any of our three main authors or any of
you–make of the various points raised by our two commenta-
tors, Ulric Neisser and Ross Day?

6

DIFFERENT BRICKS, ONE TOWER

THEODORE E. PARKS

University of California at Davis

First of all, I am intrigued by Ross Day's challenge that reconciling the diverse beliefs of our three main authors may not be realizable. I'm not so sure. (I will, however, grant that the reconciliation I want to propose may not be a "theory" but, rather, a way of approaching perception—a "tool kit" of ideas, if you will.)

Take his amusing example of the tiny figures of Laurel and Hardy. To me, this is a wonderful example of Irv Rock's idea that seeing is, at least sometimes, a problem-solving activity. The "problem" here is that there are two possibilities: What's out there is either small people in an ordinary chair *or* ordinary people in a very large chair. Why, then, do we come up with the former "solution"? I think it's because a vast warehouse of past experiences tells us that small people (children) in adult-size furniture is a common occurrence, whereas seeing outlandish-sized furniture is not. This, of course, is also a prime example of the importance of knowledge that Richard Gregory emphasizes.

To appreciate the importance here of our knowledge of the (approximate) standard size of chairs, imagine Laurel and Hardy sitting on some object that does *not* come in a standard size—say a tree trunk or a boulder. In that case, they would look normal, and we *know* they would because all of us have seen hundreds of pictures of people in just such surroundings and, of course, they *did* look normal. So, both Irv Rock's and Richard Gregory's ideas may apply here.

Things get even more convivial if we imagine that, rather than looking at Ross Day's still photograph of Laurel and Hardy, we are actually watching the movie he found so hilarious. One thing we would notice (as surely he noticed) is that the boys not only look small in a frozen "glance" but also *stay* small as they move about in the giant set. One possibility that many psychologists would favor is that our visual system *prefers* to see things as having a constant size (unless there is strong evidence to the contrary). After all, most things in nature do not change size over the short term, so we may have evolved such a preference as a good "first guess." This, of course, is an example of the sort of "sideways-in" rule that Richard Gregory also favors, but there is another possibility. Suppose we see our two actors from a raised camera angle and suppose the flooring on which they are standing has some regular pattern—say, a black-and-white checkerboard motif. In this scenario, an interesting fact would emerge as they moved about: The relationship between the size of their feet on the screen and the size of the squares they are standing on would always remain the same (i.e., it would be "invariant"). This is exactly the sort of thing John Kennedy and Ulric Neisser have in mind when they emphasize the importance of "higher-order invariances." Furthermore, this explanation is *completely* compatible with the "preference" idea; both could contribute.

But why believe that invariance matters? Another thought experiment helps. Suppose, by some computer trickery, we managed to alter the film so that every time Laurel or Hardy moved away from the raised camera, the tiles got larger. My guess is that, in this doctored film, the actors would appear to shrink! This is only a guess—someone really ought to try this—but I'd bet on it.

The point of all this is that the various beliefs of the various authors in this book may coexist *as long as* none of them claim that anyone else is completely and always wrong, which they don't. To me, rather than anyone being right or wrong, the real issue is which ideas apply in which situations. Better yet, the issue ought to be the *relative* importance (again, depending on the situation) of various factors that contribute together. After all, good accurate perception might be good *precisely because* it is the end result of multiple, mutually supportive contributions.[1]

So, for example, people who believe that a good deal of preconscious inferring is often necessary are free to agree that various invariances occur in nature and that they may be important and may even reduce the need for inferential "leaps" in some cases. They may, in fact, proceed to determine which ones matter when. On the other side, those who emphasize such variables are equally free to admit that, under relatively impoverished conditions, a good deal of unconscious detective work might be required and might actually occur. And to my mind, we all should embrace them both; it might not seem like as much fun as feuding, but it's better psychology.

Now, having said that none of the authors completely rejects the ideas of any of the others, it must be admitted that Ulric Neisser comes close to doing just that—and gives the new reader the best idea of the heat that some debates can generate—so his views should be carefully noted. Specifically, he is dissatisfied with, among other things, Irvin Rock's explanations of the Ames room and apparent motion effects and Richard Gregory's proposed understanding of the appearance of the "hollow mask," the former for involving supposed inference and the latter for supposedly involving top-down knowledge. Neisser is almost certainly correct in arguing that recognizing a face as a face is a "special case," but surely what the process entails, then, is some sort of *inborn knowledge*. So his real disagreement with Gregory is only over how many such special cases there may be, an obviously worthwhile question. Similarly, his objections to Rock's proposals are not as dogmatic (or isolating) as they may seem, except in the best philosophic sense; he is arguing for *theoretical economy,* that we must not multiply mechanisms (assumptions) beyond what is *necessary*. What this means in Rock's two cases is that we must not assume that the visual system makes unconscious assumptions or inference *unless* we can't explain the same phenomena without them. I think we can all agree that such open-minded skepticism is good for the health of our field.

Having said that, however, it seems to me that Irv Rock would respond that such assumptions *are* sometimes necessary. In the case of the Ames room, for instance, the optical projections to the retina are, as Neisser points out, the same as those that would come from a rectangle viewed "straight on," *but* they could also come from a variety of walls of other shapes at other angles (including the actual one in the distorted room). How do you choose which one to "see" if not by an assumption?

But Neisser is still right: We should always think long and hard about what is in our retinal images ready to be simply taken in.

BUT IS ALL OF THIS "INTELLIGENT"?

Both Ulric Neisser and Ross Day prefer not to label most (or any) of the activities of our visual system as "intelligent" on the grounds that (a) its application is limited and (b) it doesn't help.

While I agree that using such a label adds nothing to our understanding of precisely how vision works, I would cast my vote with the majority (especially if we stick to the definition given at the outset of this book). Such a label is, to me, a very convenient way of reminding myself how dramatically good vision usually is, a point on which all of us seem to agree.[2]

Of course, "a word is just a word," but this one carries an important rallying cry: Let's find out *how it is* that we're so good.

NOTES

1. Rather ironically, the same may be true of strong illusions; they may affect so many people so much because they, too, are multiply determined.

2. To appreciate how this point is perhaps *the* major point, consider for a moment the fact that, as you look around you, you are not in direct contact with any of the objects you see. Rather, you are in intimate contact *only* with a set of electrochemical events going on inside your skull. For example, if the external world were suddenly to cease existing, your experience would not change one iota, *provided* that these activities in your head continued! That's impossible, but it's certainly interesting—and *important*—to think about.

PART III

Their "Further Looks"

In these final chapters, ideas that were developed in each of the first "talks" are explored in more depth, often with additional points that are interesting in their own right (but somewhat more technical), for those who simply want to know more.

7

A FURTHER LOOK

Two Stages of Perception

IRVIN ROCK

There is still another argument I would make in favor of a problem-solving view of perception. It concerns the hypothesis that the perception we typically end up with is the result of "stages of processing." The first stage achieves an organization that corresponds closely with the patterns on the retina. For example, given a stimulus like that of Figure 1.2 (in Chapter 1), that organization consists of only black regions, and the three-quarter circles are seen as such, not as amodally complete and overlapped by a triangle. There is no depth, and there are no amodal regions. I call this the "literal percept" or the proximal mode of perception. It simply correlates, region by region, with the retinal image. Similarly, the literal percept in Figure 1.1 would consist of two halves of a horse separated by a rectangular region (although without the recognition of these halves, the percept might be more accurately characterized as a rectangular object with irregular protrusions on both sides). In other words, we are aware that we are *not* seeing the central region of a long horse.

By contrast, if I see a woman approaching me from across a room, it would obviously be incorrect to say that she seems to get larger as she gets nearer. Obviously not! Yet, as we all know from the similarity of eye to camera, the size of the "picture" of an object formed on the back of the eye is inversely related to the object's distance. Therefore, by the time she reaches the middle of the room, her image on my retina has more or less doubled. But that does not lead me to see her as larger and larger. We refer to this kind of phenomenon as "constancy": The perception remains remarkably unchanged (it remains constant) despite the fact that the stimulus reaching the eye, which one would *think* ought to govern the perception, is quite variable. Constancy also implies a further fact about our perception—namely, that it is typically accurate or correct or "veridical."

On the other hand, the literal or proximal mode stage of processing yields a percept that is closely correlated with the stimulus on the retina. So we *are* aware that objects at a distance *do* take up a smaller region in our field of view. And, by the same token, if an object is very near (e.g., if you place a hand close to your eyes), you are aware that it fills your entire field of view (although it still may appear to be "hand size").

An interesting, closely related point is that, when you are trying to draw an accurate picture, you want to draw distant objects as smaller than objects of the same size that are nearer. In other words, to draw a proper perspective, you have to access the proximal mode. This is because, to "work," the drawing has to be like the retinal image or a photograph. Of course, this is difficult to do for most people, though artists can do it easily (although you may sometimes see an artist holding up a pencil or finger against the object he or she is trying to draw to get its image size correct). This is because *constancy* is so *dominant*.

What has happened is this: The literal percept is followed—in most cases, almost instantly—by a second stage of processing that results in what is the *preferred* percept. I call this the "world mode" (as opposed to the literal "eye mode") of perception, and it is, of course, the one I have had the most to say about. For Figure 1.2, the preferred percept is of a white triangle in front of complete, partially amodal circles; similarly, for Figure 1.1, the preferred percept is of a long horse, the center of which is seen amodally, covered by a blue rectangle. In general, the preferred percept usually entails the perception of at least some degree of depth and constancy, which are, of course, facts of the world.

THE IMPORTANCE OF TWO STAGES

There is evidence supporting this two-stage hypothesis, and so it is surprising that the existence of the literal percept stage has been so overlooked. Much of the evidence is anecdotal but well-known to investigators of perception. For example, transparency effects, such as those shown in Figure 7.1, are not necessarily seen immediately, and before such a perception is achieved, one often perceives instead a mosaic of regions of varying lightnesses:

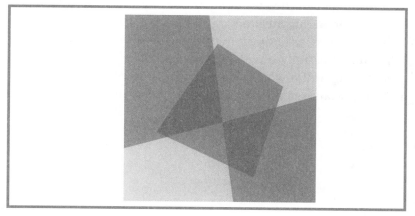

Figure 7.1. Transparency Effects

Another kind of evidence for the reality of the literal percept is, as I have just noted, the fact that it is often still perceivable even as one is achieving the preferred percept. For example, one might say that, in all cases of amodal perception, we are perfectly aware of the fact that the amodal region is not visible (i.e., is absent). As I have said, in the case of constancy, in daily life we often simultaneously perceive in the proximal mode as well as in the constancy mode.

What is the importance of these two stages or aspects of perception? To begin with, they provide a better description of the way the world looks to us than does a description based entirely on the constancy or world mode. For example, according to the constancy mode, when standing in the middle of a railroad track or long road, one should perceive the tracks or edges of the road as perfectly parallel and the railroad ties as equal in size all the way to the horizon. In a sense, that is a reasonably correct description, but, in another sense, it is not. We also see the tracks or road as converging, and we see the wooden ties of the railroad as getting progressively smaller. This latter way of describing the scene is in the proximal mode. It is quite like the retinal image if we could see it, and it is quite like a photograph of the scene. In short, there is a dual aspect of our perception, and, even granted the dominance of the constancy mode, we should not leave out either mode in our musings.

Nevertheless, as I hope is now apparent to you, I believe that it is in our successfully traversing the gap between these stages—in our arriving at the world stage—that we reveal to ourselves the truly important realities that must be "grasped" by vision.

8

A FURTHER LOOK

Tactics for Detecting Illusions

JOHN M. KENNEDY

Thus far, we have chiefly considered settings in which accurate perception occurs. But, as Irvin Rock mentioned, we are prone to errors of various kinds. I would add that perception needs tactics for detecting them. Consider geometrical illusions.

Geometrical illusions, such as that in Figure 8.1, are ones that use lines and contours on a page to induce misperception of lengths, curvatures, and areas:

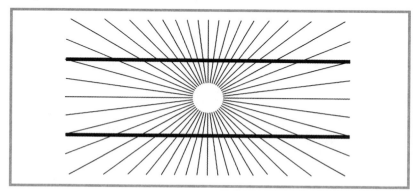

Figure 8.1. Geometrical Illusions

We have an impression that the two large lines in the figure are bowed outward. They are, in fact, straight and parallel. Interestingly, I have found that if the page carrying the figure is tilted so that the display is viewed from a low glancing angle, the apparent curvature vanishes; the lines appear straight and parallel. That is, the illusion can be dispelled by tilting the page away and, thus, viewing it from a low angle. The reason the illusion is dispelled is that it depends on lines radiating from the center that cut across the two parallels at *acute* angles. These acute angles project more *obtuse* angles when the display is tilted, so their illusory effect is much weaker.

Viewing the display straight on and then at a low angle produces two radically different impressions. To have somewhat different impressions of an object from different vantage points around a display is perfectly common, but it is rare that the two impressions directly contradict each other. Normally, the set of vantage points around an object provides *commensurate* impressions—ones that fit together and provide a more complete percept of the object. But this figure yields incommensurate impressions. The display's two large lines *cannot* be *both* parallel and bowed outward.

Information has to be accurate or it is not information. So if information is obtained from two different sources or two different vantage points, it should be commensurate. Each lesson learned about a feature of an object, if it is based on information, should reaffirm the previous lessons. The fact that there is a discrepancy indicates that an illusion *must* be present.

Another illusion occurs in Figure 8.2, in which two curves appear to be of different sizes. My students and I found that this illusion—known as the Jastrow C shapes—persists if the two C shapes are cut from two separate pieces of paper and are switched in full view of the observer. That is, the upper C shape can be moved down below the other one, and it will promptly look like the larger of the two C shapes. Even small children then exclaim that the two shapes must be equal in size. Optic information for constant properties of objects consists of invariants in transformations. Here, the exchange in location of the two shapes is the transformation that yields the informative invariant; the difference in size depends purely on their relative locations.

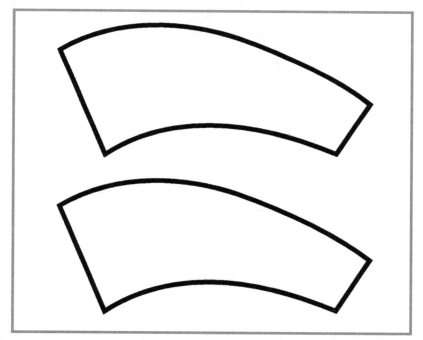

Figure 8.2. Jastrow C Shapes

To uncover a discrepancy, the observer can change a vantage point or exchange parts of the display. At times, the discrepancy can be made evident simply by adding a feature.

Rubin (1915) described Figure 8.3 as a paradox. The bottom half of the line to the left looks shorter than the line to the right, but the two horizontal lines look parallel. If the figure is shown without the upper line, the paradox is not evident, but as soon as it is drawn, a little attention reveals the contradiction. As Rubin put it, the figure is "incompatible with geometry."

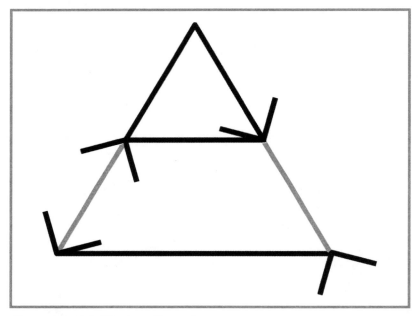

Figure 8.3. A Müller-Lyer Illustration

Rubin's figure uses a Müller-Lyer illustration, caused by arrowheads or Vs attached to lines. For reasons that are as yet still obscure, these Vs can elongate or shorten lines. What *is* clear about illusions like this figure is that they can be combined with other lines to create inconsistencies in perception.

Taken together, these figures show that three kinds of transformations tell us that illusions are present. In one transformation, the display is seen from several vantage points. In a second, one part of the display moves with respect to the others. In the third, an element is added. All these transformations provide patterns of effects that are inconsistent. I have called this the "mu" principle: Distortions combine in additive and inconsistent ways, while information, being accurate and error-free, can only combine in consistent ways.

The dual nature of perception is evident in these effects with illusions in a subtle but useful way. Any given, individual momentary impression can be misleading, but the set of effects across transformations contains information that reveals that error is present. However, the set of effects does not dispel the momentary impression. Both persist. The observer may well be in full possession of a set of effects that indicates what the true state of affairs is, but the illusion evident at a given vantage point can still be present in strength. The set of effects can give rise to a clear awareness that two lines are parallel, or two regions are the same size, or two target lines are equal in length, but the illusions persist that the parallels are bowed, the regions are unequal, and one target is longer than the other. Awareness, it seems, does not cast out illusion. It merely discounts it.

9

A FURTHER LOOK

Inside the Black Box

RICHARD L. GREGORY

Physiology and artificial intelligence (AI) have generally emphasized bottom-up processing rather than top-down, which often is almost entirely ignored or rejected. This may be because bottom-up processes have been much easier to investigate physiologically. Only recently have noninvasive brain-scanning technologies made it possible to get reasonably direct measures of cognitive brain processing. Although technologies can provide new knowledge, and are often highly suggestive of models for how to think, limitations of technology can distort and inhibit understanding.

LOCALIZING BRAIN FUNCTION

The nineteenth-century phrenologists thought that there were brain functions directly related to personal attributes that were located in certain regions and, when highly developed, gave palpable bumps to the skull. Although highly misleading, this notion has not altogether died out. More than 30 years ago (Gregory, 1963), I wrote the following:

> It might be interesting to consider how an electronic engineer deals with, and represents, specific functions in a complex device. He uses three types of diagrams to represent an electronic machine. There are (a) *blue prints,* showing the physical locations in space of the components, with their sizes and shapes; (b) *circuit diagrams,* in which each component is shown in diagrammatic form with its connections; and (c) *block diagrams,* in which there are a number of boxes connected together with flow lines, each box being labeled with its function.

Points a, b, and c are quite similar to David Marr's (1982) well-known three levels of description in his book *Vision,* though I was not implying digital computing. I continued,

> If a part is removed from a complex machine, we do not in general find that simple elements or units are now missing from the output. . . . The functional processes taking place in the components, or groups of components, of a machine are generally quite different from anything in the output. Thus we do not see the spark in a car engine represented in its output—we see wheels turning and the car moving: no spark. If a component is removed almost anything may happen: a radio set may emit piercing whistles or deep growls, a television set may produce curious patterns, a car engine may backfire, or blow up or simply stop. To understand the *reason* for these behavioral changes we must know at least the basic principles of radio, or television, or car engines, or whatever it is, and also some of the details of the particular design.

This goes on:

> Thus the removal of any of several widely spaced resistors may cause a radio set to emit howls, but it does not follow that howls are immediately associated with these resistors. . . . In particular,

we should not say that the function of the resistors in the normal circuit is to inhibit howling. Neurophysiologists, when faced with comparable situations, have postulated "suppressor regions."

These are criticisms, or at least warnings of dangers, of ablation experiments for localizing brain function. They do, however, allow that separate systems (e.g., the notes of a piano) can be identified from ablations, so brain modules can be established. Since this was written (more than 30 years ago), the visual system has been found to be modular: processing of form, of color, of movement, of stereopsis, and so on being individually carried out in specialized regions. Within a module, it may well be true that, as I said, "It would seem that ablation and stimulation data can only be interpreted given a model, or a 'block diagram', showing the functional organization of the brain in causal, or engineering, terms." So, it still seems to me that what is needed are conceptual models for interpreting perceptual and other brain processes to see with understanding inside the black box. What we need is *theoretical neurology.*

ANALOG OR DIGITAL?

Is the brain analog or digital, or perhaps a hybrid? By "digital," I mean *going through* the *steps* of a calculation. By "analog," I mean *avoiding* calculation by selecting some system that has appropriate input-output relationships. We do speak of "analog computers," but I think this is a conceptual mistake. Analogs avoid the need for computing. They are (though not always available) alternatives to computing. The same is true of look-up tables, logarithms, or reading off answers from graphs. Looking up a logarithm or reading off a graph saves having to compute. Similarly, a leaky electrical capacitor can be used as an integrator without actually performing the mathematical procedures of integration.

It is important to note that, although one may *describe* the capacitor with a mathematical algorithm, it does not itself *use* algorithms to derive the answer. Here lies vast confusion!

An implication is that it is inappropriate to call the early stages of vision "computational" if visual filters and the like do not compute. Brain physiology appears to be utterly unlike a digital computer. It now seems clear that the nervous system works by analog means, the slow components providing rapid, if somewhat rough and ready, answers.

It is often held that any defined process can be carried out by digital computing. But this needs qualification. The stresses and strains of a bridge can be represented in a computer, but the computer cannot be, or actually make, the bridge. This has an immediate relevance to artificial intelligence. Even when analog processes are reproduced in digital computers, it does *not* follow that the computer can actually do the same tricks. For example, it may be too slow. Thus, if the brain consists of many analog modules, serving to avoid having to compute thousands of differential equations every time we see or pick up a teacup, then it may be impossible to make a corresponding robot without introducing similar noncomputing analog modules. This would not be a digitally controlled machine, and the analog modules might be hard or even impossible to analyze completely in computer terms. This is not so important. What is more important is that, even if we can analyze and completely understand physiological and cognitive processes, we may still fail to make really effective AI machines to implement our understanding with digital computing. Also, if an AI simulator fails actually to function, it may simply be incomplete. This implies that practical success in AI is not necessarily a test of theoretical advances.

The distinction between *describing* with a computer model and *creating* vision with a computer is fundamental, though often confused. We can see the difference very clearly by considering something outside biology or AI, such as the Earth going around the sun. Kepler and Newton described this mathematically, but it in no way follows that the Earth computes its own orbit. The Earth is not a mathematician, but mathematics is needed by us to describe what the Earth does. Exactly the same might be true of the brain. Indeed, it seems to be implausible that the brain has to *compute* for vision. Many of the early low-level processes we know about certainly are not computed. It is most unlikely that lateral inhibition at the retina is given by computing (though computer models may well be used to describe lateral inhibition under various conditions; then modeling the individual filters and how they are related may give deep understanding). But to turn this around, to make an eye with digital filters may not work in practice, because, at least, biological components are so slow. Considering the cortex, processing speed is critical when there are combinatorial exponential explosions of possibilities (or for searching through large ensembles); thus, speed can determine what is possible or impossible. It may be that modular organization, with dedicated fast processors, helps to avoid disastrous combinatorial explosions of possibilities. Such considerations seem important for relating AI solutions for suggesting how we may see inside the black boxes of the brain.

Electric recording from single cells has proved perhaps surprisingly informative, notably for vision (e.g., the Nobel Prize-winning work of Hubel and Weisel, 1968). Now noninvasive techniques detecting neural brain activity, though indirectly via increased local blood flow, are starting to throw new light into the black box relating physiology to cognition. To cite one recent finding, using positron emission tomography (PET), Alex Martin and colleagues (Martin, Haxby, Lalonde, & Wiggs, 1995) at the U.S. National Institute of Mental Health showed black-and-white line drawings of several objects and asked subjects to name a color or an action associated with each object. Brain regions close to regions associated with color vision lit up when color was imagined; those close to movement areas lit up when action was imagined. They conclude,

> We always see things in terms of the meaning they convey. . . . That's how we identify them so quickly. . . . This is a step from physiology to bring meaning to the study of the brain. . . . We further suggest that the perception of objects and their written names automatically activate a widely distributed network that includes the areas active during colour and action word generation, as well as sites that mediate knowledge of other object attributes. Activation of this network occurs without conscious effort and lasts for only a brief period of time.

So physiological and cognitive research are, indeed, converging.

REFERENCES

Adrian, E. D. (1928). *The basis of sensation.* London: Christophers.

Broad, C. D. (1929). *Mind and its place in nature.* London: Kegan Paul.

Dennett, D. C. (1991). *Consciousness explained.* Boston: Little, Brown.

Ellis, W. E. (Ed.). (1938). *A source book of Gestalt psychology.* London: Routledge & Kegan Paul.

Falletta, N. (1983). *The paradoxicon.* New York: John Wiley.

Gibson, J. J. (1979). *The ecological approach to visual perception.* Boston: Houghton Mifflin.

Gregory, R. L. (1963). Distortion of visual space as inappropriate constancy scaling. *Nature, 199,* 678-691.

Gregory, R. L. (1966). *Eye and brain.* New York: World University Library.

Gregory, R. L. (1970). *The intelligent eye.* London: Weidenfeld and Nicholson.

Gregory, R. L. (1980). Perceptions as hypotheses. *Philosophic Transactions of the Royal Society B, 290,* 181-197.

Gregory, R. L. (1987). Intelligence based on knowledge—knowledge based on intelligence. In R. L. Gregory & P. K. Marstrand (Eds.), *Creative intelligences* (pp. 1-8). London: Frances Pinter. (Reprinted in 1987, *Interdisciplinary Science Reviews, 12,* 3, 211-215.)

Gregory, R. L. (1994). The unnatural science of illusions. *Proceedings of the Royal Institution of London, 54,* 93-110.

Hershenson, M. (Ed.). (1989). *The moon illusion.* Hillsdale, NJ: Lawrence Erlbaum.

Hubel, D. H., & Weisel, T. N. (1968). Receptive fields, binocular interaction, and functional architecture in the cat's visual cortex. *Journal of Physiology, 196,* 215-243.

James, W. (1890). *The principles of psychology.* New York: Holt.

Kellman, P. J., & Shipley, T. F. (1991). A theory of visual interpolation in object perception. *Cognitive Psychology, 23,* 144-221.

Kennedy, J. M. (1974). *A psychology of picture perception.* San Francisco: Jossey-Bass.

Mach, E. (1959). *The analysis of sensations and the relation of the physical to the psychical.* New York: Dover.

Marr, D. (1982). *Vision.* New York: Freeman.

Martin, A., Haxby, J. V., Lalonde, F. M., & Wiggs, C. L. (1995). Discrete cortical regions associated with knowledge of color and knowledge of action. *Science, 270,* 102-105.

Morgan, M. J. (1977). *Molyneux's question.* Cambridge, UK: Cambridge University Press.

Neisser, U. (1967). *Cognitive psychology.* Norwalk, CT: Appleton-Century-Crofts.

Neisser, U. (1976). *Cognition and reality.* New York: Freeman.

Parks, T. E. (1989). Illusory-figure lightness: Evidence for a two-component theory. *Perception, 18,* 783-788.

Petry, S., & Meyer, G. E. (1987). *The perception of illusory contours.* New York: Springer-Verlag.

Rock, I. (1983). *The logic of perception.* Cambridge: MIT Press.

Rock, I. (1995). *Perception.* New York: Scientific American Library.

Rubin, E. (1915). *Synoplevede figuren.* Copenhagen: Gyldendalske.

Ungergleider, L. G., & Mishkin, M. (1982). Two cortical visual systems. In D. J. Ingle, M. A. Goodale, & R. J. W. Mansfield (Eds.), *Analysis of visual behavior.* Cambridge: MIT Press.

Warren, W. H., Mester, D. R., Blackwell, A. W., & Morris, M. W. (1991). Perception of circular heading from optical flow. *Journal of Experimental Psychology: Human Perception and Performance, 17,* 28-43.

Webster's new collegiate dictionary (2nd ed.). (1956). Springfield, MA: Merriam-Webster.

INDEX